The New W
Using the E   Methodology

# DESIGNING
# TRANSFORMATIVE
# EXPERIENCES

A **Toolkit** for
**Leaders, Trainers,
Teachers,** and other
**Experience
Designers**

BK®
Berrett–Koehler Publishers, Inc.

**Brad McLain, PhD**

Berrett-Koehler Publishers, Inc.
1333 Broadway, Suite 1000
Oakland, CA 94612-1921
Tel: (510) 817-2277
Fax: (510) 817-2278
www.bkconnection.com

ORDERING INFORMATION

**Quantity sales.** Special discounts are available on quantity purchases by corporations, associations, and others. For details, contact the "Special Sales Department" at the Berrett-Koehler address above.
**Individual sales.** Berrett-Koehler publications are available through most bookstores. They can also be ordered directly from Berrett-Koehler:
Tel: (800) 929-2929; Fax: (802) 864-7626; www.bkconnection.com.
**Orders for college textbook / course adoption use.**
Please contact Berrett-Koehler: Tel: (800) 929-2929; Fax: (802) 864-7626.

Distributed to the U.S. trade and internationally by Penguin Random House Publisher Services.

Berrett-Koehler and the BK logo are registered trademarks of Berrett-Koehler Publishers, Inc.

Printed in the United States of America

Berrett-Koehler books are printed on long-lasting acid-free paper. When it is available, we choose paper that has been manufactured by environmentally responsible processes. These may include using trees grown in sustainable forests, incorporating recycled paper, minimizing chlorine in bleaching, or recycling the energy produced at the paper mill.

Library of Congress Cataloging-in-Publication Data

Names: McLain, Brad, author.
Title: Designing transformative experiences : a toolkit for leaders, trainers, teachers, and other experience designers / Brad McLain, PhD.
Description: First edition. | Oakland, CA : Berrett-Koehler Publishers, [2023] | Includes bibliographical references and index.
Identifiers: LCCN 2022051391 (print) | LCCN 2022051392 (ebook) | ISBN 9781523002627 (paperback ; alk. paper) | ISBN 9781523002634 (pdf) | ISBN 9781523002641 (epub) | ISBN 9781523002658 (audio)
Subjects: LCSH: Leadership. | Experiential learning.
Classification: LCC HD57.7 .M395825 2023 (print) | LCC HD57.7 (ebook) | DDC 658.4/092—dc23/eng/20230227
LC record available at https://lccn.loc.gov/2022051391
LC ebook record available at https://lccn.loc.gov/2022051392

First Edition

30  29  28  27  26  25  24  23      10  9  8  7  6  5  4  3  2  1

Book production: Westchester Publishing Services
Cover design: David Ter-Avanesyan

To my children, Kai and Koli
Embarking on the great transformation we call Life,
Dream your dreams and embrace the changes.

# DESIGNING TRANSFORMATIVE EXPERIENCES

# Contents

# Introduction

The Nature of Transformative Experiences

> *A flock of wild geese flew over the master and student as they sat*
> *together by the stream.*
> *"What are they?" asked the master.*
> *"They are wild geese, sir."*
> *"Wither are they flying?" asked the master.*
> *"They have flown away," replied the student.*
> *"You say they have flown away," said the master, "but all the same,*
> *they have been here from the very beginning."*
>
> —Baso

What was your most transformative experience (so far)? What events were included? Where were you? Who else was there? How old were you? And most importantly, how did it change you?

Perhaps it was when you were young and fell in love for the first time. Maybe it was becoming a parent and realizing that your life was forever changed. It might be a tragedy you lived through, a traumatic injury or experience, a cancer diagnosis, or the death of a loved one that altered your self-perceptions ever after. It could be that one boss who was able to inspire you to become more than your job and empowered you to do your life's work. Or that insightful coach who drew forth untapped potential you never even knew you had. Or that special teacher who opened your eyes to a new way of seeing yourself in the world.

Transformative experiences are the most powerful events in our lives. They shape and define us. They are what we secretly crave, what we strive for, and what we cherish most, both personally and professionally. They are the events upon which our lives turn and our destinies unfold. And through us, transformative experiences can change the world.

What if we could understand how transformative experiences work across a range of human experiences? What if we could use that understanding to intentionally design "the transformative" into our lives and the lives of others? And what if we could harness this understanding for leadership—designing transformative experiences to motivate, elevate, and inspire those we lead? Imagine the possibilities for leading the way to a more positive and inspiring world.

After all, this is how we describe our very best leaders—at work, in innovation, teaching, coaching, parenting, the arts, and every other domain. Transformative leaders seem to have an innate and ineffable ability to touch our hearts, provoke our minds, stretch us beyond ourselves, and conjure experiences that change our lives and make the world a better place.

Is there a code or formula for leading in this way consciously, deliberately, and strategically? Is there a body of knowledge we can harness to become masters of this art? How can we become transformative experience designers?

While there is no singular one-size-fits-all recipe for designing transformative experiences, there is indeed a research-based method, which I present here in this book as Experience Design Leadership using the methodology of ELVIS: Experiential Learning Variables & Indicators System. But before we get into all that, we must ground ourselves in a simple yet profound truth:

Transformative experiences do not happen *to* us,
they are created *by* us . . .
whether we realize it or not.

Over the past two decades in my work as a social scientist, I've been
exploring the nature and psychology of transformative experiences
in an effort to understand what they are and how they operate.
I have been extremely privileged to work with exceptional leaders engaged in efforts that shape our world and affect all our lives—from
contributing to NASA and the Space Shuttle Program, to collaborating with Jane Goodall for over 15 years on her world conservation
efforts, to leading cutting-edge education research for the National
Science Foundation, to leading groups on international travel and
other adventures, to directing three documentary films, to working
on the psychology of leadership with some of the largest and most
influential companies in the world.

This work has led to a fundamental understanding at the core of
how transformative experiences unfold. People typically describe
their most transformative experience as something that *happened to
them* and over which they had very little control. But on closer in-
vestigation, these experiences—including what they mean in our
lives, our capacity to fully participate in them, and their outcomes—
ultimately *come from within us,* regardless of the external triggers or
circumstances. The transformative in our lives is not simply waiting
for us out there somewhere; its possibility and its potency are quietly
waiting for us in here.

Why is this? How is this? And how can we unlock this latent potential? Imagine if we could understand how transformative experiences work and use that understanding to intentionally bring the
extraordinary into our own lives? What if we could become expert
designers of experiences that propel the growth and transformation
of others, whether we play the roles of leaders, educators, parents,
artists, or friends? Becoming skilled at the art of transformation is
to harness a life-changing tool that allows us, as Henry David Tho-
reau put it, "to live deep and suck out all the marrow of life." That
is what this book is about.

Not only have I been studying this phenomenon as a researcher, but, like most human beings, I've also been living it. As I write these words, I am recovering from cancer and COVID-19, as well as a difficult divorce after 20 years with my two young children involved, all amid the worldwide pandemic/endemic that has most of us living a "new normal." As we all sometimes do, I find myself at the intersection of several transformative experiences at once, shaping who I am and providing opportunities for me to "suck marrow" (hopefully without choking on the bone!). And I will share these and several other stories throughout this book—both my own personal stories and those of many others—as we examine transformations of many different kinds, from the tragic to the triumphant, and how we ultimately forge the meaning they will have as our lived experiences.

In my research, I define transformative experiences as **learning experiences** that have an **identity impact**, changing the experiencer's sense of self in some important way—who you believe yourself to be or who you aspire to become. In almost all cases I have studied, people describe their most transformative experiences as having multiple deep impacts that ripple through every area of their lives and are durable (or even amplified) over time. Think again of your own most transformative experience so far. Is this true for you as well?

As you reflect on your own most transformative experience, let me share with you one of mine. In the end, I suppose it can be classified as an inspirational experience, borne from tragedy. It is certainly an example of how transformation sometimes comes when life is at its most challenging. As I look back now, this is how the whole business of studying transformative experiences really got started for me.

## Origin Story: The Space Shuttle *Columbia*

As a boy, I wanted to be an astronaut, a commander of flights into the unknown and alluring dark of space in the fashion of Luke Skywalker, James T. Kirk, and Neil Armstrong. Destiny saw it differently. However, by the age of 30, the dream was still alive in me—working for NASA, working in human spaceflight, working on a mission into space! With education as my newfound life's passion, I was spearheading an experimental digital learning project: theatrical science education using live actors, virtual characters, and experiential methods to communicate science to the public. It seemed my earlier aspirations for outer-space exploration had turned to the inner-space journeys of the mind. But at least it was an exploration set in that same context of irresistible cosmos from my childhood. It was 2001. The focus of my project was the upcoming space shuttle mission STS 107 (Space Transportation System, mission number 107), whose task was to ferry seven representatives of our species into space. It was, in all respects, a dream project. I wrangled my brother, a Hollywood film producer, into the project and together we forged a relationship with George Lucas's Lucasfilm to pull off the magic. For two consummate *Star Wars* fanatics, it was a validation of the highest order, with perks: working at Skywalker Ranch, Industrial Light and Magic, and LucasArts, exchanging ideas, writing scripts, discussing technology, and meeting face-to-droid with an idol of my childhood, R2D2. The project was becoming a bona fide confluence of childhood aspirations.

But it was the shuttle crew who collaborated on the project that resonated with me in the deepest ways. Michael Andersen, Willie McCool, Ilan Ramon, Rick Husband, David Brown, Laurel Clark, and Kalpana Chawla were everything astronauts were fashioned to be: brave, sharp, and curious pioneers intent on joining with space, absorbing the emptiness, and filling it with their own over-achieving, competitive innocence. We worked closely with each of them, learning their stories, their work, their passions. Individually, they exuded a contagious thirst for adventure and daring, tempered with a healthy dash of science and inquiry. And I harbored a secret jealousy for their path, which so resembled my own conjured childhood ambition but now seemed only to highlight its remoteness from me.

Collectively, this close tribe of scientific sojourners formed the most intimate of families, and I was welcomed, if only occasionally, as a guest at the table over two years as they prepared for flight. I remember Kalpana Chawla, or KC, one of three veteran space fliers on the mission, the most. I asked her on camera one day to share with me something of the experience of spaceflight from her previous flight. She was an East Indian by birth, a scientist by training, but all heart as I was to discover.

"Spaceflight is definitely going to affect everybody differently; it's a given," she started. "One of my officemates had told me, make sure that you look at the Earth. And I took that very seriously and said, somehow or another I'm going to look at Earth for one whole orbit." She spoke in a slow and precise accented rhythm. "An orbit takes ninety minutes. Late in our flight I had that opportunity during a sleep period. And I hovered by the window and just looked at Earth for a whole ninety minutes."

She cast her enchantment on all of us in the room, effortlessly sweeping us up with her into low Earth orbit. "The continents were moving by . . . the very green Atlantic Ocean . . . and the desert comes, the Sahara. And there are landscapes, which look as if you are on Mars already." Her eyes gleamed with the dreamlike faraway gaze of a woman in love. "Then there is the Nile, which looks very much like a lifeline. You see clouds with lightning just shimmering through them because you are looking at it from above rather than below.

"Coming over to Australia and how the Great Barrier Reef looks . . . it sounds like a cliché, but Australia really wears a necklace around it." She smiled at the memory. "And during the early morning lights and the late afternoon lights, you can see shadows and sparkles and it just looks very magical. And you see a sunrise, a sunset during that time, which is so colorful—very fast, almost like a kaleidoscope.

"And then, it's ninety minutes . . . you are back where you were. And you know, it wasn't that the sights themselves weren't impressive, they were." Suddenly, we were once again sitting in the room with the camera and the lights. I struggled to shrug off the dream, the afterglow of space travel. "But what really struck me was . . . my gosh, it took just ninety minutes. To me, it's almost like a mantra that still rings." Here she paused to formulate.

"You know, you go from one place to another, anywhere, and it takes you time. And we'd gone around this whole planet . . . and this is the only place we know where life exists . . . and it took just ninety minutes! It's not a new piece of information. I knew that. But it stuck. And it really amplified the fact . . . how small this place is." A tiny Earth flashed in my mind, a mote in the sea of black. "I mean there's this whole big sky, filled with stars that seem far away, but this right below is the only place that I know that can sustain me . . . where I can feel the wind, the water . . . listen to the leaves rustling." The hypnotic sounds called me home across the void, so small in the terrifying immensity.

Again I snapped back. KC was staring right at me, imploring. "And it really personally makes you want to take care of it. It impacts you where you want to go to the people who are fighting and say, 'You know, it takes only ninety minutes and then you are past this place.'"

There was nothing to say and we said nothing. My eyes were gratefully wet with tears. As she spoke, I came to realize that KC was granting me my youthful heart's long desire—to experience space. Ironically, it was Earth that she shared, but from a new perspective. By this gift, I was now a traveler through space aboard my home world and will forevermore be. I was feeling inspired. But the real inspiration was yet to come, and I wasn't going to like it one bit.

In his epic documentary series *Cosmos* (KCET PBS TV mini-series, 1980), astronomer Carl Sagan says, "The cosmos is all that is, or ever was, or ever will be. We have lingered long enough on the shores of the cosmic ocean. We are ready at last to set sail for the stars." And it was to these words I turned for comfort all those years ago on a sunny February morning in 2003 as I watched the rain of smoke trails that once were the space shuttle *Columbia*, burning down through the sky in heartbreak. Owing to an accident on launch two weeks earlier, a hole was punched into its left wing and the orbiter disintegrated upon reentry, just 16 minutes from landing. It was the end of *Columbia*, the beginning of the end of the shuttle era, and the end of my project and three years of my life. But most painfully and senselessly, it was the end of *Columbia*'s crew.

For months I dreamed of them. They would gather around me in blue flight suits and black boots and tell me, "It's all right, Brad," that I had "done well," and that they were proud of *me*. Words I longed to hear, I suppose, yet strangely unhealing in their irony; it was of course *they* who had done well and of whom I was proud. They would circle around me, sympathetic hands on my shoulders. KC would shrug easily and smile.

Then I would awake, struggling again to justify their deaths, trying to make peace with a blown-apart faith in the direction of our space program, for which they had paid too dearly. If they could've somehow known the tragic outcome, I wondered, would they themselves have traded their lives for this mission, for this science?

In that year of dark depression in the aftermath of the accident, I slowly came to realize something. I don't think they would've traded their lives for this mission, and I don't believe they did. But they were willing to *risk* their lives. They were willing to risk their lives for something larger than themselves, for a human future in space. To be a part of that vision, to contribute to that, they were willing to take the biggest risk anyone can—to give all they had to give. And that is exactly what they did.

What was I willing to give my life for? What risks was I taking to make a difference in the world? What was my contribution? Shaken by their example, I decided to "ante up" that year and, like them, become as expert as I could be in *my* sphere of exploration: education, identity development, and experiential learning. I decided to make a contribution, to go back and get the PhD, to do the research, to push the limits of my own field, and to take the risks. And all along where I could, I wanted to share the story of the *Columbia* crew, to whom my debt will remain unbalanced. It was a confused, difficult, and at times painful process for both me and my family. But, as we shall repeatedly discover throughout this book, transformative experiences often are. As a result, however, I learned. I was inspired. I was changed.

## ELVIS Is Born

As time passed, I became increasingly curious about what I had experienced, the process by which it had changed me, and how *any* experiences that change us really work. I began looking into it, deeply. It stretched me. Ultimately, the quest led me through education research, psychology, identity theory, design, even poetry, and, most critically, ground-truth practical experience in the real world.

One day several years ago, I was asked by my dear friend and producer Shaun Harner to do a TEDx talk on my work. In it, I told the story about my time in the Space Shuttle Program (a part of the story I shared above) and then very briefly presented my theoretical framework for researching transformative experiences. I ended with a final story about applying the framework in my travels leading groups to Tanzania, Africa, and wound up going way over my allotted time. After the talk, however, I was inundated with questions I could not answer: How can I use your framework for . . . inspiring my employees, designing curricula for my students, creating museum exhibits, making movies, coaching my team, enhancing my own training programs, designing adventure travel, raising my kids? Designing, inspiring, creating, making, enhancing—these were the questions I got. I realized that while I apparently did a great job of exciting people about the psychology of transformative experiences, I failed to deliver on the particulars of *how* to design for them practically and all that entails—the learning, the design variables, the indicators of transformation. The notes of ELVIS slowly began to form and resonate in my mind.

I spent the next two years unpacking the implications of my framework. I plunged into the existing research on the practical design and use of the theories (there was shockingly little). I continued original research on designing transformative experiences and led such experiences for hundreds of people from all over the world. Sometimes the experiences I designed involved exciting adventures in faraway places. Sometimes they involved rare or once-in-a-lifetime opportunities. And sometimes they involved what appeared to be normal everyday happenings, but for an extraordinary (if hidden) internal context. Through it all, I methodically sought to reveal the elements common across all transformative experiences, regardless of their details. I focused on understanding how transformative experiences work cognitively and emotionally, but now specifically on how I could use that understanding to assemble the tools needed to intentionally *design* such experiences in very practical terms, and help others to do so as well.

So what did I learn? Transformative experiences come in as many different forms as the people who have them. Although they are subjective in nature (e.g., what may be transformative to me may not be transformative to you), there are indeed common denominators of these uncommon experiences. Not surprisingly, the single most significant shared factor across all transformative experiences is, of course, our human psychobiology. For whatever the variation, specific content, or different types of transformative experiences we might consider, we find consistencies that are due to the ways we perceive our experiences, the processes by which we translate our perceptions into knowledge, and the manner in which we forge new meaning and understanding about ourselves and our world as a result.

I synthesized these consistencies into a practical system, and because transformative experiences are universally **learning** experiences, I dubbed it *ELVIS*:

*Experiential Learning Variables & Indicators System*

ELVIS is the foundation for Experience Design Leadership. It includes a framework for understanding how transformative experiences work and a design toolkit with seven key experiential design elements and the ELVIS Design Matrix.

But there's more. It's not just our human psychobiology that helps explain these commonalities and the reason why ELVIS is so powerful. The human heart is central to the questions of how and why transformative experiences occur.

> It demands an inner courage from us to examine who we are in the world and who we will become.

It demands an inner courage from us to examine who we are in the world and who we will become through the various pathways, choices, and intentions of our lives. The heart is where this spirit to venture beyond ourselves resides. And this spirit has been both revealed by and made possible by the transformative experiences of nearly everyone I have worked with in studying this phenomenon.

Finally, although I use the language of ELVIS Experience Design Leadership in this book, let me clarify an important point. Since transformative experiences are subjective to each individual and ultimately emanate from within, I am talking about designing *opportunities* with high probability for having a transformative experience. The elements and tools of ELVIS are intended to create the *optimum conditions* and frame of mind for transformative experiences to occur. You, as the designer, present the doorway. Your experiencers will have to walk through it themselves. But you also provide much more than just the doorway. You offer the room, the furniture and decor, the lighting, and everything else too. As the experience designer, you are the leader, architect, interior designer, and personal host. Designing transformative experiences is, to paraphrase the poet David Whyte, to generate an invitation for people to enter into a new conversation with themselves on the fiercer frontiers of life (*The Invitational Identity*, online talk, November 8, 2020). You as the leader do not control that conversation. You do not control the transformation, although you help to guide it in a positive direction. As an ELVIS Experience Design Leader, you invite others to one of the most precious opportunities that we have in life: to author our own change journeys in becoming better versions of ourselves.

## Who Is This Book For?

I can't tell you the number of leaders I've spoken with recently who've expressed the desire to go beyond their traditional leadership roles of managing people and processes, beyond simply meeting the next deadline or quarterly targets and revenues, beyond performance reviews and promotions and policies. There is a growing thirst for something deeper, and it's coming to the surface in the COVID era. It's about knowing how to work and how to lead on deeper levels.

Leadership for personal transformation is what this book is all about. Wherever mentor-protégé relationships exist—from business leaders to teachers, parents, entrepreneurs, coaches, trainers, and others—if you seek to become skilled in leading transformative experiences for those in your charge, this book is for you.

Here we will translate the rich and fascinating psychology of our most important life experiences into an entirely new view of leadership. It is a view that recasts leaders as *experience designers* and explores the enormous potential that this paradigm shift opens up for transforming lives and empowering those we lead with the fire of self-propelled identity growth.

This is an opportunity to move beyond leading organizations, projects, and processes to more clearly see the people in our spheres for who they are, rather than merely their job roles. And this is an opportunity to reexamine preconceived notions about who a leader is supposed to be. This is an opportunity to apply social science research to reinvent yourself as someone who can lead deeply rooted personal change.

Importantly, this book also applies personally to each of us as we lead our own lives. For in order to design transformative experiences for others, we must first cultivate this capacity for ourselves. That is where effective ELVIS Experience Design Leadership always begins.

## How the Book Is Organized

Part 1 of the book lays the foundation needed to understand ELVIS—the **ELVIS Framework**—and wield it effectively. We will tap into research revealing how our neurobiology is hardwired to translate our experiences into rich narratives, and how those narratives can be intentionally structured to frame transformative events. We will discover how our transformative experiences are powerfully shaped by the risks we take, including those that are unconscious. We will examine how our ideas about who we are determine not only the kinds of experiences we *can* have but also how our identities are *changed* through our transformative experiences. And we will breach the elusive psychology of inspiration, the holy grail of transformative experiences and a phenomenon describing some of the most sublime and misunderstood experiences in human life.

Then in part 2 you'll unpack the **ELVIS Toolkit**, including the ELVIS Design Matrix and the ELVIS 7, the seven elements of transformative experiences. Each of the ELVIS 7 will be presented in its own chapter and will include specific design questions, examples, and strategies to immediately begin using ELVIS for your own designs.

Using the research-based strategies in this book, you can dramatically increase your capacity to design and deliver experiences that can change lives. Because transformative experiences ultimately come from within, you will learn to design experiences that empower your experiencers to become more self-aware and intentional authors of their own life trajectories, well beyond the specific boundaries of any given experience. The ELVIS Framework and Toolkit will help you become a transformational leader, able to touch hearts, provoke minds, and unlock the extraordinary in our lives.

PART ONE

# THE ELVIS FRAMEWORK

# 1 ■ ELVIS Overview

*Sometimes we are lucky enough to know that our lives have been changed, to discard the old, embrace the new, and run headlong down an immutable course.*

—Captain Jacques Cousteau,
*The Silent World*

*You're probably better off if you just shut up and play.*

—Elvis Andrus,
American baseball player

It is the heartbeat of ELVIS Experience Design Leadership, and so I repeat it often throughout this book: *transformative experiences are learning experiences that have an identity impact, changing*

A transformative experience is one that has an identity impact, changing the experiencer's sense of self.

*the experiencer's sense of self in some important way.* It is the identity component that drives such experiences and makes them internally generated, no matter the external circumstances or triggers that may surround or initiate them. This makes them different from any other significant or extraordinary experiences in our lives.

In defining a transformative experience this way, several questions emerge that are important for leaders wishing to learn how to design such experiences:

- In what *way* is an experience transformative?
- Are there different types of experiences or types of transformations?
- *How* transformative was a given experience?
- Is there a continuum or some kind of 10-point scale for *transformative-ness*?
- So what if you have a transformative experience? What *difference* does it make in your life or in the world?

The answers to these questions vary widely because transformative experiences are subjective in nature, which makes perfect sense if their source is internal to us. Therefore, on the surface, transformative experiences can look very different from one another, depending on a wide range of experiencers and experiences and whether they are designed or undesigned, initiated by external events or driven by internal ones.

When we look closely at the nature of transformative experiences across this wide range, certain commonalities emerge. First, they all track through the same basic sequence of stages. And while not a code or a formula, this sequence composes a *framework* for understanding how transformative experiences operate and how we can become skilled designers of them. This is the ELVIS Framework.

Recall that ELVIS stands for "Experiential Learning Variables & Indicators System." The ELVIS Framework is the underlying structure of the system. There are three components to the ELVIS Framework, which we will unpack in the next three chapters. They are as follows:

1. *Discomfort zone experiences,* which include experiences of many different kinds but that invariably incorporate personally relevant learning about ourselves and the worlds we live in
2. *Narrative translation of experience,* which is the way we convert our experiences into personal understanding and make meaning from them
3. *Identity construction,* our dynamic and constant process of becoming, which determines who we are psychologically, as well as what we do, what we think we can do (or even attempt), who we aspire to be, and how we transform

The framework works like this (see figure 1): Transformative experiences fall into different *discomfort zones* (the subject of chapter 2) according to their details and circumstances—events, themes, context, and other internal and external factors. Ultimately, we translate these experiences into narratives of different kinds, something that we are naturally quite good at and that our brains are hardwired to do (precisely how and why is the subject of chapter 3). Our most powerful experiences are translated into our most important narratives. If these experiences and their resulting narratives are important enough, they become part of our *identity narratives.* Identity

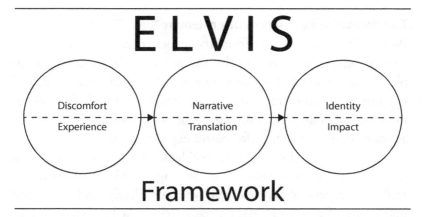

**Figure 1:** Experiential Learning Variables & Indicators System

narratives (the subject of chapter 4) live in that very special and carefully guarded library of volumes within our heads that contain our most personal and valuable possession: our sense of self. These are the stories that inform who we are, how we experience life, what we can do (and what we cannot do), and who we want to become. When an experience alters our sense of self through this process, it becomes a transformative experience, and it has the power to change our lives from within, the lives of others, and the world beyond.

Think again of your own most transformative experience so far, but now see it through the ELVIS lens. What discomfort zone elements were included? What kind of narrative did you construct from it? How did the experience, through that narrative, change your sense of self?

Understanding the details about the three main components of the ELVIS Framework (the subject of the next three chapters) unlocks a powerful design platform for creating these kinds of experiences as leaders in many domains, and even for ourselves.

But of course, there is more. Emerging from the ELVIS Framework are additional commonalities that help us further understand the broad-stroke nature of transformative experiences and give us insight on how best to design them. Here I will highlight two of the most important: "bake time" and "life invitations."

### Transformative Experiences Often Require "Bake Time"

Part of the nature of transformative experiences is that they often require some "bake time" for this full process to happen. For example, the space shuttle *Columbia* tragedy I described earlier stretched me into several discomfort zones over time, including feelings of being lost, sad, angry, fearful, and disillusioned, variations of which are quite common in transformative experiences.

On the very eve following the accident, a CBS news crew was in my house interviewing me about the tragedy. My attempts to describe my experience at that time were completely inadequate and inarticulate. I did not have the perspective or the language to make meaning of it all so suddenly. Looking back now, I understand my early lack of narrative clarity as a kind of necessary ineptitude. It was the forging fire required for me to properly narrate what I was experiencing and how I was changing in a way that would guide me through it. Only after I surfaced from the postaccident period almost a year later did I recognize myself as someone else, as fundamentally changed.

Think of an experience you've had that changed with bake time. Maybe it's the way you think about a school experience from way back, a current or past relationship, or a significant job change. Perhaps it's an adventure you had or a group experience you shared with others. We often notice these kinds of bake-time changes best by examining how we tell the story: the setup, the plot points, the details, and the conclusion. What stories of yours have you changed the telling of as you've gotten older? It often takes weeks, months, or even years for people to make meaning from their most powerful experiences.

Importantly for leaders who design transformative experiences, bake time suggests that the most critical stage of an experience—the deeper inward journey—is still occurring even

> The most critical stage of an experience is still occurring even after the most observable parts are over.

after the externally "designed" or most observable parts are over. It also tells us that transformative experiences are dynamic over time, with meanings that evolve as we integrate them into our larger life narratives and grow older (and hopefully wiser). They do not stop when the primary designed experience is "complete."

Despite (or maybe even because of) our best-laid plans as experience designers, eventually our designed transformative experiences take on a life of their own. Ultimately, the leader must step aside and give the design away to its unfolding in the hands of those who live it and who must therefore narrate it. When this happens, a new and very

> Ultimately, the leader must step aside and give the design away to its unfolding in the hands of those who live it.

personal dimension of the experience is budding—and it is a very good sign. The very best we can do as designers is to recognize this important moment in the process and accommodate it, help structure it when we can, but also let it fly when the wind of it meets the new wings the experiencer has grown.

### Transformative Experiences Are Life Invitations: What I Learned from Cancer, COVID, and Divorce

The moment you're told that you have cancer is a transformative experience. Whatever your hard-won or intricately assembled identities might have been before this moment, in an instant a new and unwanted identity bursts to the top of your priority list: "cancer patient." For me, it was a truly surreal moment, indelibly changing my sense of self and an example of life offering me an invitation that was, at first, very hard to see.

I was conducting some leadership workshops at Apple, at the Apple One headquarters in Cupertino, California. The facility is a beautiful round building of glass about the size of the Pentagon, and locked down with incredibly tight security. Escorts were required for visitors like me to even walk to the restrooms. We had just broken for lunch and were moving into the hallway when my phone buzzed. I recognized the number as my doctor, and I knew she had my biopsy results. Not wanting to take the call in front of my workshop participants or team colleagues, I spied someone just leaving their little office a few doors down. As the office door slowly started to close, I hustled over and managed to slide my foot over the doorjamb just in time and ducked quickly and quietly inside. Certainly it was a breach of the rules, but I hoped my friends at Apple would forgive me for seeking a moment of solitude.

"I have your results," she said. "It is a malignancy. You have cancer." I felt a trapdoor open beneath my feet. Down I went, falling into myself. My doctor continued on with additional details and next steps, but after the cancer proclamation, all I heard were distant and unintelligible words, as if in a foreign language and far away. What is that old saying, that each of us is only a single phone call away from our knees? This was that call for me, as I slowly slid down the glass window to the floor, to my knees.

My heart and mind were racing one another at warp speed. I began to sweat. And then very slowly, very gently, a singular silence descended on me. I remember looking out that window into the middle of the donut-shaped building, where an external green park was, and thinking, "How simple and lovely is this scene." Time slowed. Leaves swayed in the breeze. Birds flew in slow motion. I became numbingly detached. I felt like I was observing someone else living this moment, not me. It was what psychologists call a state of temporary depersonalization, not uncommon during high stress or shock. For me, it marked a threshold crossing from the familiarity of my prior existence and my prior self into a new life by way of an extreme discomfort zone—the first component of the ELVIS Framework.

When I emerged from the room, I announced the news to my colleagues, "I have cancer." And in simply uttering those words myself, my detachment was over. It suddenly became true. Those three words became one of the shortest and most important narratives in my life—the second component of the ELVIS Framework. And with that, I instantly became a cancer patient and took on a new identity— the third and final component of the ELVIS Framework.

It was a transformation that I was all too conscious of happening in real time. It was also the fastest whiplash experience of ELVIS I have ever known. As I said, transformative experiences often require bake time, almost like water seeping through rock. But sometimes they bake fast, striking like lightning!

Put another way, if the ELVIS Framework were a baseball diamond (see figure 2), how quickly you round all the bases depends on what kind of hit sets you running. In this case, the hit was a deep fly ball to left center field and then continuing on right out of the park that sent me around all the bases in a single shot, a most unwelcome home run.

After years of unpacking and examining hundreds of rich and complex transformative experiences from people across all walks of life through my research (including the intricacies of their

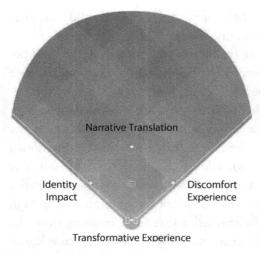

Narrative Translation

Identity
Impact

Discomfort
Experience

Transformative Experience

**Figure 2:** Baseball Analogy

discomfort zone experiences, the variations and layers of their resulting narratives, and the multifaceted identity impacts that formed their ultimate outcomes), here I was faced with a mind-blowingly simple, inescapable, and heart-wrenching reduction of the entire ELVIS Framework in its starkest, meanest terms. The full cycle in a matter of minutes. I was in awe of life's powerful hand and the fragility of my stability. What I did not know then, and what all cancer patients reading this will know all too well, was that it was only the beginning of a series of transformative experiences. They would seismically ripple through the landscape of my sense of self from the epicenter of that time and place, in that little room, in Apple One.

Whether sudden like the crack of a bat or slowly evolving with lots of bake time, the fundamental nature of any transformative experience is that it is an *invitation* life is making to us. Oftentimes, as with injury, tragedy, or illness (as was the case for my cancer), it is an invitation we cannot refuse. However, we can decide the manner in which we will RSVP.

Looking back on the events following my cancer diagnosis, I can more clearly see the invitation life was offering. Cancer was an ambassador of change for me, ushering in a new season of my life by asking me to turn away from the past I had known and the person I had been, and turn to a future I had not expected or was prepared for. It was an invitation to live differently by accelerating the frontier of my own mortality. It brought me into real conversation with myself about the life I had been hoping for versus the life I was actually living. And it starkly highlighted what changes I needed to make. This "frontier accelerating" nature of transformative experiences is always inviting us to reconfigure ourselves and our relationship to life. In

> This "frontier accelerating" nature of transformative experiences is always inviting us to reconfigure ourselves and our relationship to life.

my case, many invitations subsequently flowed forth from my cancer diagnosis.

First, it laid bare the cracks in my 20-year marriage and led to its heartbreaking but ultimately inspirational unraveling. With that came an invitation to set my heart free after years of unacknowledged self-imprisonment. Cancer also invited me to redirect my career priorities toward my "passion work," of which this book is a part. It also sparked an invitation to rekindle a long-neglected yet deeply treasured friendship I thought I had lost. And perhaps most deeply, it brought forth an invitation to change my identity as a father from someone expected to have all the answers to someone guiding and sharing in the asking of life's beautiful questions alongside my two children, even if sometimes scary.

All these invitations occurred for me just as COVID was ramping up as a global pandemic. On the still-raw heels of my recovery from cancer and in the midst of my divorce, the utter weirdness of my own internal life was externally echoed in the weirdness of the new normals of the COVID world: isolation and quarantines, closings and lockdowns, mask wearing, hand sanitizers, scrubbing down our groceries, homeschooling, rampant illness, clogged hospitals, and rising death tolls. The media airwaves became saturated with all kinds of COVID-related coping advice precisely as I was struggling to put my life on a new track. I could easily close my eyes and imagine all this helpful guidance was intended just for me. All I had to do was turn on the radio to get "three self-care tips for getting through the day" or turn to social media for the latest "COVID stress-management steps to follow this week." They might as well have had my name on them: "How to deal with isolation and uncertainty . . . for Brad."

Like hundreds of millions of others, I was infected by COVID during the writing of this book. COVID is a transformative experience that is continuing to change all our lives, for some much more than others. On an individual level, it has been an unwanted (but perhaps much needed) invitation for each of us to take a hard look in the mirror and ask ourselves some fundamental questions: Who am I right now? What am I doing and why am I doing it? Is this who I want to be? At the same time, COVID has also invited us to take a deeper look outside ourselves and become more keenly aware of the struggles and transformations it has ushered in for different people in different ways. Collectively we know that already marginalized groups, including racial and ethnic minorities, have suffered more in terms of both life impacts and death rates due to COVID. Women have shouldered much more of the burden of pandemic childcare, online homeschooling for their kids, and other home-based tasks that disproportionately interfere with their careers and life balance. We know that the poor, aged, and immune-compromised are at much greater risk for all the negative consequences of COVID in every category.

When we see these differential impacts revealed in the lives of our friends, family, and neighbors, we are reminded of the intersectional nature of transformative experiences. Our transformative experiences, of any kind, occur at the intersection of all the other contexts, currents, and eddies of our lives occurring at those moments. These life contexts include our identities going into such experiences and our life circumstances *at that time.* Therefore, as leaders designing transformative experiences for good ends, we must recognize that any invitations we might make to our experiencers will land very differently with different people owing to this intersectional nature of transformative experiences; these experiences cut across our many identities. This is both a challenge for us as designers and a blessing, but in both cases a wonderful reminder that we are unique in our self-configurations and that we are, each of us, living lives never lived before in the entire history of history. The future is open wide to us.

## Exercise

Cast yourself as a social scientist for the moment and unpack your most transformative experience using the ELVIS Framework. In what ways was your transformative experience a discomfort zone experience? How do you tell the story of this experience, and how has your telling of it changed over time? How do people close to you tell the story about your changes from their perspectives? How did the experience narrative change or inform one or more of your identity narratives, the stories that form your sense of self? Looking back, we can also now ask, what would you change about your experience if you could? This brings us into the mind of a designer. Keep this and other examples of your transformative experiences in your mental library. They will prove invaluable as you begin to lead by transformative experience design.

Share your stories! Visit the companion site for this book at DesigningTransformativeExperiences.com to find the Transformative Experience Forum, where you can share your own stories and questions about Transformative Experience Design with the community of ELVIS designers.

# 2 ■ This May Hurt a Bit

Seeking Discomfort Zone Experiences

*I could not have done anymore. I had pushed myself to a limit that I had never touched before and that's definitely going to change you.*

—Elvis Stojko,
Canadian Olympic skater

*The human journey is a continuous act of transfiguration. If approached in friendship, the unknown, the anonymous, the negative, and the threatening gradually yield their secret affinity with us.*

—John O'Donohue, *Anam Cara*

As we have already seen, our most transformative experiences simply do not occur in our comfort zones. They do not happen in the reassuring, familiar, and safe spaces of our lives. Rather, they happen in the brave spaces, the unfamiliar, good and bad. They demand

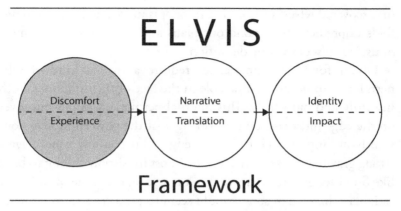

**Figure 3:** Experiential Learning Variables & Indicators System

we explore and embrace the unknown, the new, and often the difficult, both in the world outside and in the world inside us. This is where we often discover the richest experiences of our lives. Discomfort zones are precisely where transformative experiences occur. Discomfort zone experiences are the first part of the ELVIS Framework for designing transformative experiences (see figure 3).

When people talk about getting "out of their comfort zones," they are talking about vulnerability. Think of the last time you felt truly vulnerable. Perhaps it was great worry for your own or your family's health during the pandemic. Maybe it was an embarrassing event in full view of colleagues or professional peers. Perhaps you had to admit to something you were not proud of that could jeopardize your future. Maybe it was a time of sheer terror when you were physically afraid for your safety or the safety of someone you love. Maybe it was a time you revealed something about yourself or your feelings to someone new in your life. If you're like me, maybe it was simply the last time your teenager borrowed the car to go out with friends.

Generally speaking, we do not like vulnerability. We avoid it when we can. We struggle with it when we have to. We minimize or eliminate it wherever possible. And yet, vulnerability traces that razor-edge frontier between life's more severe experiences and our own undiscovered selves. Life on that frontier is unmapped and often unfolds unpredictably, beyond our plans and expectations. For most of us, it is discomfort by definition.

Discomfort zone experiences require a special kind of self-permission to become vulnerable in the face of the unknown, both inwardly and outwardly. This internal permission to put ourselves on the edge must constantly work against the powerful forces constantly pulling us back from that edge. Our comfort zones have a strong gravity well, seductively and almost irresistibly calling us back like Siren songs into what we think is safe, appropriate, positive, or rational. These Siren songs would seem to protect us from vulnerability and take the form of "responsible" habits of mind, justifications and skills for avoiding risk, and internal voices disguised as wisdom that point out all possible fears and dangers. To stand on the frontier of a discomfort zone is to confront these accumulated forces head-on, and it is no small matter.

When my children were small, they loved hearing poems by Shel Silverstein. One of our favorites speaks directly to this internal tug-of-war. The poem is "Listen to the MUSTN'TS." Maybe you know it. It is one of those classics that grow up with you and work on many levels.

In the poem, Silverstein speaks of resisting those voices that tell us what we cannot and should not do, and then invites us to expand our possible futures by reminding us with the closing line that "Anything can happen, child" (*Where the Sidewalk Ends* [New York: Harper and Row, 1974], 27). Removing our self-limitations to vulnerability is the first step. However, this also includes dealing with "toxic positivity." Society places an intense pressure on us to feel happy and positive all the time, even in the face of difficult, negative, or uncomfortable situations or experiences. Through such cliché one-liner life philosophies as "Just stay positive" or "Everything happens for a reason" or Monty Python's "Always look on the bright side of life," toxic positivity is another method of avoiding discomfort zone experiences and the vulnerability that comes with them. ELVIS Experience Design Leaders need to recognize toxic positivity as a hollow form of encouragement that should be avoided, even when well intended. At its worst, we need to identify it as a way experiencers avoid struggling with discomfort zone experiences. We then can provide opportunities for them to authentically and intentionally grapple with their discomfort. Or as a colleague of mine likes to say, "stand in the muck."

At the same time, embracing discomfort for the purpose of growth and transformation is not at all the same as saying, "If you are feeling uncomfortable about something, you are doing it right." That is most certainly wrong. Seeking discomfort for the purpose of discomfort would be a mistake, in my view. For any feelings of discomfort we might have about an experience may indeed be well founded and need to be listened to and analyzed. Sometimes internal gut feelings or intellectual objections arise precisely to keep us safe.

ELVIS Experience Design Leaders need to help experiencers articulate the difference between healthy discomfort, which warns us and protects us, and unhealthy discomfort avoidance, which keeps us from growing because of irrational fears of vulnerability. This requires some knowledge of risk psychology, or what I call "risk calculus" in my ELVIS designs, to ensure the risks we take are strategic and not reckless or misguided (covered in chapter 6).

As ELVIS designers, we serve as compassionate ambassadors of healthy discomfort, intentionally building the kinds of experience designs that ask experiencers to confront their fears and vulnerability and to engage exactly where "thar be dragons," beyond the edges of the map of their known experiences. And as the experiences we design become harsher and more difficult, they require more vulnerability for people to fully participate in them.

We are compassionate in this work because we know that the Siren songs of our comfort zones, while offering a certain veneer of safety, can also unintentionally lead us into seasonless worlds of disengagement and numbness. And we know that vulnerability, far from being a liability to minimize, is the vehicle to the discomfort zones where learning, growth, and change occur. The self-permission our experiencers need in order to inhabit this vulnerability comes in the form of carefully calculated risk. Therefore, our design tools for discomfort zone experiences are strategic risk, uncertainty, and a compass pointing to a healthy versus unhealthy form of discomfort, all discussed in practical detail in chapter 6. Here, however, we will set up that conversation with a broader look at the relationship between risk, discomfort, and the forms of risk that lead to transformation.

## What Kinds of Risk Are Transformative?

As noted screenwriting teacher Robert McKee would teach his students about dramatic structure and motivation, "We give the highest value to those things that demand the highest risk—our freedom, our lives, our souls" (*Story: Substance, Structure, Style, and the Principles of Screenwriting* [New York: ReganBooks, 1997]). Our sense of risk has an inverse relationship to our sense of agency. Agency is our power to affect an experience as an agent of change. Our sense of agency is how aware of that we are. It is what we believe ourselves to be capable of. If something is low risk for us, we have a high sense of agency that we are capable of handling whatever it is. We feel more comfortable and confident, sometimes even a bit more than we should. Alternately, if something is high risk for us, we have a low sense of agency that we are capable of handling it and we feel uncomfortable, vulnerable, or fearful. What we perceive as risky for us describes our vulnerabilities and defines our personal "discomfort zones."

> What we perceive as risky describes our vulnerabilities and defines our "discomfort zones." This is where we discover the richest experiences of our lives.

There are four critically important kinds of risk in the ELVIS Framework that appear in nearly every transformative experience: physical, emotional, intellectual, and social.

- Physical risk: These are situations that put our bodies in harm's way, like astronauts sitting atop a fueled and smoking rocket, fighting in a war, free-climbing a high cliff, or even a child learning to swim or ride a bicycle. Physical risk includes uncertainty that we will emerge whole and healthy. Physical risks also present opportuni-

ties to increase our physical capacities and have new
sensory and kinesthetic experiences.

- Emotional risk: These are situations that put our hearts on
  the line. They expose us to emotional and spiritual uncertainty and make us vulnerable to heartbreak, loss, feelings
  of rejection, exclusion, or being lost. They also present
  opportunities for us to experience empathy, compassion,
  and spiritual insight in ourselves and others.
- Intellectual risk: These situations challenge our strategic
  and rational minds. They include problems and problem
  solving that require our knowledge, our creativity, and our
  capacity to assess, learn, and adapt. These situations hold
  consequences (good and bad) for our continued intellectual growth, self-esteem, and overall well-being.
- Social risk: These are situations that test our connections
  to others, including our close, intimate relationships, our
  family dynamics, our affiliations with colleagues, our
  communities, and other more durable or even transient
  social cohorts. Social risks make us vulnerable to losing
  our healthy connections and/or building unhealthy ones,
  or even failing to make new connections. But social risks
  also present us with opportunities to forge new positive
  attachments to others, raise our standing in social circles,
  and have new social experiences.

Of course, in discomfort zone experiences, these different types
of risk are never neatly sorted like this, but rather mashed together
in a dynamic dance of commingled perceptions and realities. While
it's tremendously useful to parse them apart when investigating how
transformative experiences work, and certainly for designing such
experiences, it is also important to consider how they are synthesized
in the minds of experiencers. And all this has to do with how we
perceive and interpret risk.

Perceived risk in each of these categories is more important than
actual risk or even risk outcomes in most cases. The higher the
perceived risk, the greater the perceived challenge, the lower the
sense of agency that we can succeed, and the deeper we go into

our discomfort zones. As ELVIS designers, this is just where we need to lead our experiencers—into places where they must make risk decisions.

## Discomfort Zone Experiences Require Risk Decisions

If I had to imagine my most uncomfortable hypothetical scenario, it would likely involve being sick, being unable to help people I care about or myself, or simply being very afraid. Joe Hughes had all three at the same time in his most transformative experience, on Mount Everest—the mountain the Nepalese people call Chomolungma, or "Goddess Mother of the Universe." In many ways, Joe's Everest odyssey was a carefully designed experience gone completely wrong, something not uncommon on Everest.

Joe had studied and prepared for years to do this climb. He had trained and conditioned himself to be self-reliant, independent, even heroic with a bit of arrogance thrown in for good measure. After the first week of the climb, his climbing guides had remarked on how well he handled himself on the mountain and noted his skill with the gear. They were impressed with his endurance and his "go get 'em" attitude. In every way he could, he brought the anticipated challenges of Everest into his comfort zone.

Joe's original and highly detailed plans included several meticulously designed risk decisions. These included when to climb, who would be on his team, what gear to use, when to clip in to guide ropes over deep crevasses at the expense of speed for safety, whether and when to use oxygen, and a hundred other "smaller" risk decisions such as when to push on, when to rest, and even what food to eat and when. Some of these kinds of decisions may not seem to represent much risk to us in everyday life, but they are elevated to high-stakes risk status when climbing the world's highest mountains.

Had it gone according to design, Joe would've fulfilled his lifelong dream to reach the summit. Atop the summit he had planned to ask his girlfriend and climbing partner to marry him. He was planning to pack the engagement ring in his down coat pocket for the most triumphant moment of his life. However, just before the climb, they learned that she was pregnant. Although Joe and his girlfriend were elated, she could not climb. Still, Joe went forward with his plans to summit. For Joe, climbing Everest was all about taking charge of his own destiny and fulfilling his dreams. Joe would join the many others for whom Everest represented a conquering feat of strength and shear will. But just below Camp 3, at 23,000 feet above sea level, everything changed. Joe got altitude sickness, and he quickly found himself faced with a series of unplanned risk decisions in a desperate fight for his life.

Joe's first unplanned risk decision was something far too many past climbers failed to recognize or made the wrong choice about and paid for it with their lives: when to turn back. At first Joe thought his altitude sickness would clear up if he descended a bit, and he might still have a chance to summit later on. But when his symptoms got worse even upon descending, he made the very difficult decision to give up the summit.

Even so, by the time he reached the treacherous and constantly shifting Khumbu ice fall near the base, his motor control and coordination were gone. His guides were manually helping him place his feet on every step. It took all day. When he finally arrived at base camp, he completely collapsed and had to be carried the last two hours to the medical tent.

In high altitude pulmonary edema (HAPE), the lungs fill up with fluid that leaks into the breathing spaces from millions of microscopic capillaries. Joe was near death, hypothermic, and literally drowning in his own blood when he finally arrived at Dr. Luanne Freer's volunteer emergency medical tent. Her first actions were to warm him in a thermic shell and pump him full of meds and fluids. And yet his conditioned worsened. "This is about as close to death as I've seen someone from HAPE," she later reflected. "I didn't think Joe would last the night."

Joe's next risk decision was to agree to an emergency evacuation by helicopter. In the thin atmosphere of Everest, helicopter landings are exceedingly dangerous. Base camp was already littered with the crashed remains of the last helicopter to attempt it the year before. But he desperately needed to get to lower elevation as soon as possible and determined the danger of not doing so outweighed the danger of helicopter blades cutting into the sparse air at more than 15,000 feet. Dr. Freer made the call for the helicopter, but a sudden, violent storm dashed all hope for that. The pilot radioed to say that he could only make it as far as the village of Lukla, several thousand feet lower. "Fuck that!" said Joe between violent frothy coughs. "They've got to come here. I can't make it. I can't walk to Lukla. I can't walk at all!" Joe made the next risk decision: rather than attempt the journey to Lukla and risk dying on the trail in the storm, he decided to stay put and risk dying overnight in the tent.

The storm hit. The tent rippled loudly and buckled in the wild winds. The electric generators keeping the medical tent working failed and had to be restarted multiple times. Joe fought to stay alive all through the night, struggling to breathe and coughing up buckets of bloody sputum, while Dr. Freer continued to pump meds and fluid into him and warm his severe shivering with thermal blankets and hot water bottles. She even put Joe into a portable hyperbaric chamber, known as a Gamow Bag, to virtually lower his altitude and allow him to breathe, only to have the chamber unexpectedly explode with Joe inside. The 24-hour ordeal left him dangerously depleted and even closer to death.

With no break in the weather and on Dr. Freer's last-hope advice, Joe made his final risk decision: to ultimately rely on the skill and daring of four Sherpas to save him. They wrapped Joe in a sleeping bag and took turns "wearing" him like a giant backpack as they ran him down the mountain through the blowing snow until they got to Lukla, where he was able to be stabilized at the lower altitude. Dr. Freer kept him alive, but that decision and those Sherpas saved his life. It took Joe over a month of recovery in Katmandu in order to be healthy enough to go home, and another year after that to fully recover his life.

Joe's experience was the subject of a documentary film I directed many years ago, called *Everest E.R.* (forerunner to the Discovery Channel's reality series of the same name). At the time, I thought what better place than the tallest mountain in the whole world to confront the biggest challenges and most transformative experiences in the world, right? At least, that is what I used to think about trans-formative experiences, and this is what a lot of people still think. It's why they go there, why they are attracted to Everest, and why we have a perennial parade of movies, books, and TV shows that chronicle the high drama of the world's highest mountain. Survival stories like Joe's are a staple of transformative experiences because they hinge on one of the biggest fears and risks in our lives—death itself. And not just your average run-of-the-mill death (if there is such a thing), but dramatic death.

For Joe, his experience on Mount Everest was decidedly not what he had planned or hoped for. His failed attempt to climb Earth's highest peak set into motion a series of discomfort zone events (to put it mildly) that ultimately transformed Joe in much deeper ways than if he had successfully attained his summit goal. How? Through the series of *risk decisions* he had to make. It turns out that all trans-formative experiences hinge on risk decisions. As a result, the Joe who began climbing Everest was very different from the Joe who came down the mountain.

The unplanned risk decisions he faced were smack-dab in the middle of his discomfort zones because they involved losing every-thing he had hoped for: his self-determination, his control and achievement, and his independence. He had to utterly depend on others for his survival. Joe reached a personal summit on Everest that had nothing to do with the top of the mountain but everything to do with finding his place and his humanity in a mutually support-ive community of others. He lost his arrogance and found his family, even naming his newborn daughter after Dr. Luanne Freer. Joe now serves as an inspirational speaker sharing his transformative experi-ence far and wide.

While death-daring extreme examples like Joe's may be instruc-tive of how transformative experiences nakedly work, one need not go to such extremes as climbing Everest or seeking amazing adven-tures to have transformative experiences. Why? Because risk and dis-comfort, key components of transformative experiences of any kind, are all around us and available to us every day in the form of risk opportunities. As we often explore in my workshops, people can have a transformative experience simply walking to the local coffee shop. You could get that new job or stretch assignment at work that changes your entire trajectory. You could meet your love on a hiking trail. You could be asked to volunteer for an important but difficult cause that alters how you see your place in the world. You could be faced with an enormous loss or an unexpected opportunity that changes your plans dramatically and demands changes in you.

But an important part of our job as designers of transformative experiences is to craft and embed risk opportunities (or what I like to call "risk invitations") into the discomfort zone experiences we create for our experiencers. For each risk invitation, a response is called for. A risk decision needs to be made. And while both designed and undesigned risk journeys may indeed be consistently available to us in the world all around, a critical question is, Are *we* available for the journey?

## Discomfort Zone Experiences Are Both Inner and Outer Risk Journeys

To grow and learn in any sense whatsoever is a journey through change and discomfort. Here is where leadership through transformative experience design shines. Insightful experience designers are not only able to recognize the elements of discomfort zone experiences but can help shape and sequence those elements as they guide people through the journey of living them.

In medieval times in Europe, spiritual seekers would go on personal pilgrimages to holy places or shrines to earn salvation or forgiveness, to be cured, or to help reveal life's inner and outer mysteries. In China and Japan, wandering monks of the Zen tradition would undertake long quests from master to master in search of enlightenment, seeking that one teacher who could answer their question and unlock a new level of consciousness. Typically, these journeys were framed in terms of the local religious beliefs and traditions of the region: Buddhism or Christianity or Judaism or Islam, and others. What they all have in common is the idea of a significant outer physical journey that is actually a sacred inner journey, inviting a deeply rooted change in us and our relationship to life. And this is what they have in common with transformative experiences.

I myself was recently walking the ancient Sacred Way up to the Temple of Apollo at the Oracle of Delphi in Greece. For generations, many thousands of people had journeyed here to query the oracle— as legend has it, an elderly woman propped on a tripod above a rocky crevice spewing somewhat toxic fumes—for sage advice, prediction, or wisdom. By way of reply to these desperate questions, one of her typical nuggets of cosmic insight was "Know thyself" (translation: "What are you asking me for?"). A reminder that, regardless of our long journeys, transformation always comes from within.

To engage in a transformative experience is to embark on an inward pilgrimage that can be defined as an encounter between life's harsher horizons (invariably where discomfort, uncertainty, and vulnerability preside) and the center of your own being. The physical climbing of Mount Everest or the months-long pilgrimage to a holy place is a metaphor for this inward journey. As someone embarking on a transformative experience, one needs to ask the question, What pilgrimage

> What is the inner journey that will bring you into contact with the unknown frontier while also returning you to the very source of your own self?

within yourself is needed to meet the frontiers of your life where meaningful change can occur? Or put another way, What is the inner journey that will bring you into contact with the unknown while also, ironically, returning you to the very source of your own self?

Designers of transformative experiences must guide experiencers to these kinds of self-reflective questions as we also help people live the outward metaphor of the journey in terms of risk opportunities. What kind of risk invitations and risk journeys are we talking about as ELVIS designers? As I said, one need not go to such dramatic lengths as Joe's Everest adventure to encounter transformation. Consider Tabitha's personal pilgrimage as an example that dispels this myth.

*What I Learned about Personal Pilgrimages from Tabitha the Traveler*

Tabitha's story is a designed experience that, like Joe's, includes some emergent elements that were certainly undesigned, but also provides an example of how risk journeys are available and accessible to us all in everyday circumstances, and how the inner journey becomes the wellspring of transformation.

Tabitha was in her mid-30s when her marriage fell apart. As a mom of two young boys, she busied herself with the many distractions and duties of single parenthood to numb the pain and feelings of being lost within her own life. To make ends meet, she worked as an English as a second language teacher for adult immigrants during most days, many nights, and even weekends. She found a boyfriend as a security blanket. Together, her role performances of having been a wife, now a divorcee and girlfriend, a mother, and a teacher had completely eclipsed her personal sense of self. "I remember lying in bed and having this overwhelming sense of grief, almost like when my grandmother died. But I didn't know why—who was dying? Who was dead? And then this voice, my voice, said to me— it's you. I was experiencing a bereavement of my own womanhood," as she put it, "an inner death of myself in a way."

Her younger aspirations for life included discovering her place in the world through travel, finding her passions through exploration, and making time to simply breathe and be. Who was she? Who had she become? Where was she headed? She did not like the answers that were coming back. "I came to a point where I lost track of my dreams. Was I even living any of my own dreams anymore or only other people's?" Tabitha found herself desperately needing to press pause on a life that was no longer flowing in a direction that was her own.

One day, one of her students told Tabitha of his recent travels through Europe. The hearing of his tales from the wide world beyond triggered Tabitha. She was envious of the young man, but it also empowered her own latent desire to have that experience. *Why not me?* she wondered. *Why not now?* She went home and planned out her own solo backpacking trip. Despite her nearly overpowering feelings of guilt and selfishness, as well as risking the resentment of her loved ones, she left her two boys with her parents, kissed her boyfriend goodbye, and walked out the door. For six weeks she journeyed through France, Italy, Switzerland, and Spain, encountering the world on her terms. It was not always easy; she faced a number of inner and outer challenges along the way. But as she did, she reunited with a refreshingly new yet familiar stranger: herself, reimagined.

"It was so fulfilling to see the places known only in my dreams," she said. "I learned I was stronger than I thought. I learned how adaptable I could be. How to navigate unknown cities on my own. How independent and powerful I am. But also how to trust others—and who to trust—in making my way." Tabitha's experience forged new elements of her identity. "I also learned how to be comfortable with my own perceived selfishness . . . my guilt for leaving my kids for so long but also my own guilt for NOT doing it sooner . . . not doing it for me."

When she returned home, it was clear the experience had changed her. She no longer felt defined and confined by her role as a mother. She had moved from being a spectator in her own life to being an active participant and driver. "And it was OK if I was not perfect or things didn't go perfectly. I knew I could deal with it." She felt a new sense of confidence in risk taking and in her own resilience. A ripple effect soon followed as she began to reinvent her life. She ended her relationship with her boyfriend, but doing so unafraid with the knowledge that she could take care of herself for the first time—no man needed. She quit her job, wanting something different and empowered to make it happen. She went back to school for computing and soon found a professional home that's now lasted for 25 years. And perhaps most importantly, she regained a sense of being a child of the world, free to be herself, whomever that may turn out to be.

Tabitha's most important risk decision was to go. She had to overcome her own objections and those of others. There were many other risk opportunities and risk decisions that flowed from that one: leaving her two boys and feeling like a bad mother for it, even fearing for their safety; stretching herself financially to make the trip and feeling irresponsible for it; leaving her job and her other family members and feeling extremely selfish for that; and navigating the many additional risks that come with being a woman traveling alone. But her very first decision to design and then live an outward and inward risk journey was the opening of a new vulnerability in Tabitha. And from this vulnerability, a new source of courage was made possible. In fact, it was the crux of her transformative experience. While taking risks may disturb us, alter our plans, and usher in the unknown, personally relevant risks hold the possibility to forever change us, just as with Tabitha the Traveler and Joe the Mountain Climber.

Likewise, part of our job as designers is to present experiencers with personally relevant opportunities to discover and define their own vulnerabilities and then take their own risks in service to those vulnerabilities. If our ELVIS designs are on target, they are risking *themselves* on some level, because the person returning from the mountain or the pilgrimage or the coffee shop is not the same person who began the journey. Part of us dies on such journeys, falling away like autumn leaves marking the threshold of a season as they float to the earth. And that kind of change can be quite frightening even if it is good, but much more so if the changes are unwanted or painful. But these endings create space for new births within us, new ways of walking in the world and with ourselves, and new ways of inhabiting our lives.

---

### Exercise

Think about the last time you were presented with a risk opportunity or risk invitation, either intended or unintended. What kind of risks did you perceive: physical, emotional, intellectual, social? What feelings of vulnerability did you experience? What risk decisions did you make? What risk outcomes resulted? Compare your story and answers with those of someone else, and identify the similarities and differences you discover. In most cases, common themes emerge. What are they for you?

---

# 3 ■ Storifying Our Lives

Harnessing How We Translate Experience into Narrative

*In the drape of moonbeams across a canvas of snow, the lilt of birdsong, the crackle of a fire, the smell of smudge and the echo of the heartbeats of those around us, our ancestors speak to us, call to us, summon us to the great abiding truth of stories: that simple stories, well told, are the heartbeat of the people. Past. Present. Future.*

—Richard Wagamese,
*Embers*

*Once language was available to describe social scenarios from memory and anticipations, we became "homo narratus." We have become psychological beings who are incapable of not narrating our experiences both to ourselves and each other.*

—Alan Parry,
psychologist

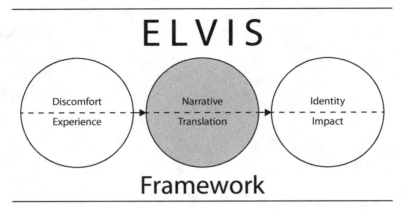

**Figure 4:** Experiential Learning Variables & Indicators System

The narrative translation of our experiences into story form is the second element of the ELVIS Framework (see figure 4). In the design of transformative experiences, we are mostly concerned with how our *discomfort* zone experiences are translated into stories, including the ways that ELVIS designers can embed and support the narration process within experience designs. But in order to get there, we must first root our understanding in the uniquely human realm of experiential storytelling. How do we "storify" our lives? It seems fitting to begin this exploration with another story.

### Narrative as a Mechanism for Transformative Experiences: What I Learned from Jane Goodall

I have the tremendously good fortune of working with Jane Goodall. I served on the board of directors for her nonprofit institute for several years, helping out on things like her Roots and Shoots service-learning program for kids, promoting her chimpanzee research in Tanzania, and helping with her conservation and humanitarian work around the globe. Now in her late 80s and still traveling more than 300 days each year (before COVID, at least), Jane is an extraordinary person. Everything you've heard about her is true. Although she appears on TV, writes books, tours the world to adoring crowds almost like the pope of conservation and science, and hangs out with celebrities to raise money and awareness for her causes, she has never become trapped by the celebrity's curse of losing touch with themselves and the world of average people. She is not surrounded by "yes" people. She is not rich. People think the money she gets for her speaking engagements goes into her pocket; it does not. It goes directly into her work at the Jane Goodall Institute. She keeps a small room in her childhood home, where she does her writing, enjoys family, and corresponds with friends by handwritten letters. She is a humble, determined, passionate, and beautiful soul, the likes of which we will not see again.

Knowing and working with her has been a transformative experience for me that continues to unfold. However, a few years back, when I was a brand-new board member, I felt somewhat lost and unsure of my place there. Although I attended every meeting and felt happy and privileged to be there, I was rather quiet and more often chose to hold back rather than rock the boat in any way with opinions and ideas that were contrary to those of other, more experienced board members. I suppose I had forgotten at that time for whom I was working—Jane herself is the ultimate "boat rocker," having single-handedly changed the science of anthropology forever and inspired billions of people with her message of conservation and compassion. I felt so inadequate to the task of being on the board that I was considering stepping aside. But one night I had a transformative experience with Jane that made my meaningful participation possible.

Jane was coming to my town, Boulder, Colorado, as one of her many stops on a tour of the United States. After a series of smaller local appearances and a huge turnout of about 10,000 people for her main event lecture, she called me and announced that she was coming over for dinner. As a proper British woman of impeccable manners, she most likely phrased it much more graciously, in point of fact, but that is what I heard in my somewhat shocked reaction. Knowing she is the frequent guest of the rich, famous, influential, and even royal, I immediately became rather self-conscious about my own private little personal world. I quickly explained to her that our house is quite small and humble—the home of two young children, two overly affectionate dogs, and an unremitting mess that migrates from room to room, but also a lot of love. "Perfect!" she said. "We'll be there in thirty minutes."

Thoroughly dumbstruck and in a panic, I called my wife (I was still married at the time) with the news. I was picking up the kids from activities, she was heading home from teaching a fitness class at the gym, and we were both thinking the same thing: "What the #$%#?" Get food and drinks, clean the kitchen and living room, feed the dogs, shower, change clothes, and oh my god, we have leather couches and the world's preeminent animal rights activist is coming to visit! It's amazing what runs through your mind in those moments. Of course, there was almost no time for anything at all. So, I ordered a bunch of Chinese food on my cell phone from the car. "Just deliver your top five vegetarian entrees and extra fortune cookies." Then, knowing Jane's taste for good whiskey in the evening, I headed straight for the liquor store with a plea for the shopkeeper: "Look, I've got an elderly British woman coming over for dinner and I know nothing about Scotch, bourbon, whiskey, or whatever. Just find me something that won't embarrass me."

Later that night, after dinner and after Jane's admonishment when I asked if I should add ice to the whiskey ("Good lord, Bradley, let me pour. You just . . . just go!"), we settled in on the back porch wearing heavy jackets and blankets under a sky flashing with the distant lightning of an approaching October thunderstorm. We swapped stories and pondered the ultimate meaning of our lives for hours. Later, I mentioned to her how I had been feeling a bit self-conscious about my smallish and untidy home (and life), imagining it through her eyes. Again, I was admonished, "Who do you think I am, Bradley? I raised my son in a tent! In the jungle!" We had quite a laugh. Ever the kind heart, she added, "This is my kind of house."

She went on to explain that she didn't know exactly who this celebrity Jane Goodall was, the individual whom people so often think of. She insisted that although she was deeply touched by the public's reception of her, the fame and attention and the legend were "not my fault," as she put it. "I don't know how this happened. I have a gift," she said. "I discovered that I can speak effectively on behalf of the animals I love so dearly, because they cannot speak for themselves. But this famous Jane Goodall 'creature' is not the real me. I'm just Jane."

Jane drove that point home a few hours later. As we were moving inside and cleaning up a bit, the rest of us noticed that Jane was missing. She had gone inside some time ago and never returned. At last we discovered her upstairs when we heard my nine-year-old son Kai saying, "Come on in a little farther, we have some beautiful spiders in here too!" Jane was on hands and knees with a flashlight, crawling into a secret fort under his bed. "I don't mind the spiders," she said. "I just don't think I can turn round again if I go all the way in!" But she did—of course she did. It was a surreal and magical night.

Whatever I had previously thought about the legendary Dr. Goodall from growing up learning all about her discoveries in the forests of Gombe, to the dozens of books and documentaries about her, to her work as a UN peace messenger and international conservationist, among the world's most recognized scientists and her mythologized, pope-like status as a symbol of hope—beyond all that, on this night, I met "just Jane." And doing so unlocked "just Brad."

In one night I went from being a mostly passive board member, unsure of my place, what I should or even *could* do, to being a member with a mission and a mandate to contribute anything and everything I had no matter how humble or unpolished. As a result, I served on the executive team for the Jane Goodall Institute, helped lead fundraising events, chaired the Roots and Shoots leadership committee for the United States, and still today try to include Jane's important work as part of everything I do, from professional speaking engagements to neighborhood pizza parties to books like this. This is what Jane does, after all. She inspires. And that night with "just Jane" changed me. But the story I just shared with you is more than simply what happened that night. The story itself is in fact the *mechanism* by which the experience changed me. Let's find out how.

## Our Narratability Conjures Our Lived Experience

The importance of narrative in our lives is hard to overstate. We have an innate ability for narration, a built-in "narratability." Humans are, quite obviously, natural storytellers and story lovers; just look at our obsession with books, TV, news media, movies, theater, story-based video games, and even the rapidly evolving ways we use social media. Narrative is the oldest, most elaborate, and preferred way humans structure our knowledge and understanding, communicate with each other, and share our lives across generations.

Beyond being storytellers, we are also consummate *story makers*. That is, we forge narratives to interpret and make meaning of the world around us and our lives within it. Through our stories we express all the passion, torment, joy, mystery, and discovery that is the human experience.

As noted psychologist Jerome Bruner put it, "We organize our experience and our memory of human happenings mainly in the form of narrative—stories, excuses, myths, reasons for doing and not doing, and so on" ("The Narrative Construction of Reality," *Critical Inquiry* 18, no. 1[1991]: 1–21). By extension, it is not at all a stretch to consider our encounters with new ideas and new people, including people long gone as well as our current relationships (good or bad), as the intersections of our mutual narratives. When strung together, our colliding narratives shape our worldviews, values, beliefs, memories, expectations, and behaviors.

We come by our narratability naturally, quite literally. There is good evidence that we are hardwired for our narrative talents. Neuroscientists have revealed that areas of the brain involved with processing narratives develop and overlap with those involved with language and higher cognition. These include areas of the cortex associated with memory, information sequencing, visio-spatial imagery, and links between hearing the stories of others and our own personal experiences.

Our cognitive skills of self-regulation and executive function are also strongly linked with our development of narrative abilities. Self-regulation describes our ability to evaluate and control our thoughts, emotions, and actions in order to solve problems and achieve our goals. Executive function refers to our higher-order cognitive skills such as adaptive thinking, time and effort management, and attentional deployment, among others.

Finally, our development of theory of mind also codevelops with our narratability. This is our ability to perceive and understand the thoughts and feelings of others. It is related to what psychologists call "perspective taking" and is the root of empathy and communication, enabling us to participate in meaningful relationships through shared narratives of self and other.

It has even been shown that the brain activity of storytellers and story hearers can sync up in what psychologist Uri Hassan at Princeton has called "neural-coupling." This has tremendous implications for leadership, persuasion, inspiring and motivating others, and building trust and commitment.

> Our narrative ability is often as invisible as the air we breathe but just as essential.

And yet, the importance of our narratability usually goes utterly unnoticed, often as invisible as the air we breathe but just as essential. In fact, the evolution of our narratability as a species tracks with our development of civilization from prehistoric times to the present. Visit the companion site of this book at DesigningTransformativeExperiences.com for a brief look at this fascinating history.

But the importance of narrative goes even deeper still. The construction of narratives is not just a description of our lives; it is actually *how* we participate in the world through our lived experiences. Our narratives are the apertures through which we experience life. They are our *living stories*. And this makes narrative creation that harnesses our innate narratability an essential tool for the transformative experience designer.

> Our narratives are the apertures through which we experience life. They are our *living stories*.

The narrative study of lives is a transdisciplinary field that examines how we translate our experiences into stories and how those stories, in turn, shape our lived experiences—past, present, and future—as well as ourselves. In my work, I have applied many of the methods of the narrative study of lives to the specific question, What makes an experience transformative? When people tell me about their most transformative experiences, they weave rich stories that I co-interpret with them. While each story is unique, I find they have certain classic narrative commonalities:

- A narrator "hero" figure at the center of a cast of characters, forging a first-order narrative from the hero point of view
- A setting of both external and internal circumstances as context
- A narrative arc or plot with a beginning, middle, and end, with a discomfort zone experience driving the action
- Specific scenes, episodes, or plot points within the narrative arc around which the story significantly turns
- A parallel character arc through which the narrator undergoes a profound change, with ripples throughout their life

These basic components provide us with clues about how to embed narrative supports into our experience designs. We can use these components to ask questions that help our experiencers structure their narrative translation process. This can cause experiencers to more consciously reflect on a project they are engaged in at work, a course they are taking, or a goal they are striving for. Let's look at an example.

### What I Learned in Africa about Narrating Change

For years I led month-long expeditions to Tanzania and places in Kenya using the ELVIS Framework. The range of transformations in people from these travels was astounding, from deeply inspiring to humbling and grounding, to gradually or even immediately life-changing. And yet, on the surface, the activities included within the overall designed experience were broadly the same for everyone: treks through the Serengeti, working with schools and AIDS orphanages, and climbing Mount Kilimanjaro (Kili).

Of course, climbing Kili (a nearly 20,000-foot volcano and the highest mountain on the African continent) was a huge and dramatic challenge for my experiencers. It was a seven-day adventure in the wild whether one successfully summited or not. Naturally, Kili was often the highlight of the experience in the stories my participants told to friends and family immediately upon their return. However, there was an interesting twist I observed: climbing Kili markedly diminished in importance with bake time after the journey was over, to be replaced by the many relationships they had forged with our in-country hosts. This ultimately changed the way I designed these experiences. To explain how, I have to begin with my very first trip to Africa as a participant under another leader.

On my first journey to Tanzania, my eyes were opened to a common pitfall when highly privileged people visit developing countries with the idea that they are "helping" somehow. Sometimes this is referred to as "white savior syndrome," although our groups were not usually all white. But it is the notion that there is an implicit disrespect and even possible damage done when well-meaning yet ego-driven travelers from wealthy countries fail to understand or care about the complexities and larger context of their hosts' home community. This was certainly true of that first group I was a part of. We were basically uninformed tourists. We brought all kinds of gifts for the kids in Tanzanian schools and orphanages, such as coloring books, markers, and educational toys that excited the kids but did nothing for their long-term benefit. Worse, it also greatly frustrated and angered their parents and teachers who could not provide those things or make much progress in improving their educational system. I was tremendously conflicted over this.

As the leader of similar journeys in later years, I was determined to change all that. My teams made a conscious effort to focus on building relationships in-country long before we actually arrived. This included collaborating with Tanzanian educators online for months before arriving, and establishing sister-school programs, contacting orphanages before our visit to learn what we could bring that *would* make a difference for them, organizing and helping our guides build and launch their own businesses and expand the kinds of experiences they offer, and maintaining those relationships for years after.

This focus on relationships fundamentally improved the experience for all involved. I observed this powerfully through the narrative-creation structures I had designed into the experience. As part of the journey, I would charge my participants with creating personal video documentaries about their experiences. The most important prompt I provided went something like this:

> *I do NOT want you to make a video about Africa. We can get any number of wonderful documentaries about Africa from National Geographic—and at a much higher quality and budget. No, what I want is the story only you can tell . . . the story no one else in the world has access to or could ever make. And that is the story about YOU in Africa and how you have changed. That means YOU have to be in your video—on camera and not just behind it—interacting with this place, its people, its animals, and with others in our group. We need to see YOUR sights, hear YOUR thoughts, and see YOU living and changing through this experience. You are the star of your video production.*

This single prompt set the stage for a first-order narrative (told from their personal point of view), the setting, the arc of the plot, and the integration of the hero arc in the form of the internal experience of the narrator.

From this simple beginning, my experiencers were unleashed on a mission to not only tell their stories in a personally relevant way but *live* the experience with their internal journey front and center to the adventure in real time as it was occurring. People loved it. The experience and perspective of making their videos *about* their journey became an integral *part of* their journey.

Often, their stories would extend well beyond the journey itself and into the impacts it had on their lives afterward (more on this in chapter 7). Many of my experiencers have gone on to use this particular technique for video creation in their own lives and work, including corporate leaders designing "off-sites," educators with their students and with each other, and even teens embarking on travel and project experiences they wished to capture and share from a very personal point of view.

Why is this approach so powerful? Once again, it taps into our natural narratability in very personal ways. It brings together those outward experiences with our own private inward journeys through personal story making. It is an integrative meaning-making process that situates us within an incredibly long and rich narrative tradition rooted deep within our biology and our cultural inheritance as members of the human race.

### What Kinds of Narratives Are Transformative?

Importantly in my work, the transformative experience stories people have shared with me fall into different narrative categories depending on the nature of the narrator's own character arc, a kind of narrative typology. These categories include the following:

- Discovery narratives and learning narratives
- Redemption and recovery narratives
- Relationship narratives
- Oppression and exclusion narratives
- Tragedy narratives
- Motivation and test-of-will narratives
- Coming-of-age narratives
- Inspiration narratives

In fact, people's transformative experiences are not typically limited to just one category, but most often fall into several, as the boundaries between categories are fuzzy, much like the categories of risk we explored in the previous chapter.

Thinking about transformative experiences in terms of what types of narratives we forge from them is a powerful design approach. It implies that we begin the experience design process with the "end in mind" by carefully considering the kind of narrative that people will translate their experiences into at the conclusion.

Thinking ahead about the types of narratives that different experiencers may generate based on our ELVIS designs, and why, is a form of Backwards Design and is a central ELVIS Experience Design Leadership perspective that guides all three ELVIS Framework components:

- How we design our discomfort zone experiences and make risk invitations
- How we embed narrative structures and supports into those experiences
- How the initial identities of our experiencers shape the kinds of identity transformations we might expect (the subject of the next chapter)

Backwards Design also applies to team leadership and the collective narratives that team members produce about an experience, as we will see next.

### What I Learned at "Big Tech" about Backwards Design

For many years I've worked with a highly effective software executive at a large computing company. Let's call her Diane. Diane's "no-BS" results-driven practical leadership approach had earned her a reputation as a dragon lady in the industry (a form of gender bias in fact). But she was legendary for expecting her team to show up in person, put in long hours at the office, and do whatever it takes to get the job done. When we first began working together through my team at the National Center for Women and IT (NCWIT), she wanted to change her team's culture to be more inclusive, diverse, and innovative. There were many options for where to start that seemed reasonable and not too risky: focusing on improving everyday experiences among her team during meetings, improving recruiting and hiring practices, or revamping performance evaluation and promotion criteria. But after we spent some time going over the social science and discussing how team culture change actually occurs, she decided to choose an area that would intentionally shock her team and send a strong message that things were about to become very different.

Diane eventually decided to start with remote and flexible work strategies, long before COVID made such a thing a necessity. It was something none of her direct reports would ever expect from her. She was right. Her team was blown away at the announcement and news quickly spread. Nobody thought she, of all people, would ever consider flex schedules and remote work as anywhere near acceptable.

In doing so, she was considering the narrative her team would come away with from this strategy: substantial rapid change. She also magnificently modeled the fact that she too was entering a discomfort zone by changing her own thinking, a vulnerable choice that served to lead the way for others. Today, Diane's reputation is as a visionary leader who is known for seeing the workplace experience through the eyes of her direct reports and someone who is willing to innovate, experiment, and take chances on their behalf. People compete to get on her team, even more than before.

This executive used Backwards Design in her decision that tracks perfectly with the ELVIS Framework: by first considering the narrative her team would construct from her decision to tackle a discomfort zone (remote work practices), and then designing an experience for her direct reports and herself to lead the way into this new mode of work, she eventually changed her team's identity from an inflexible "hero culture" (long hours in the office) to an innovative and accommodating team that recognized people's differing needs. And Diane changed her own professional identity in the process.

Think again of one of your own transformative experiences. What kind was it? Which categories does it fit into? The way to tell is to look at the story you've generated from that experience. What kind of narrative is it? Did you fall in love or take a long journey that changed the way you saw yourself? Did you suffer great loss at a young age that shaped your life from then on? Are you a cancer survivor or a war veteran? Did you become inspired by a powerful role model who changed your entire trajectory? Narrative typing is a good place to start, but it's just the beginning. What was the story arc?

What was your own character arc? What events were most critical, and how did you narrate them?

Your answers reveal not only what kind of experience you had but also how it changed you and how it fits into the larger narrative of your life as a part of the whole, or more accurately, how you've integrated it into the story of who you are and who you wish to become. The larger meaning lurking inside the narrative begins to take shape, as it likewise shapes you.

For designers, the ability to harness experiencers' natural capacities for narrative translation is the key for imbuing their experiences with transformative potential. Designers must intentionally integrate and guide the formation of the stories that experiencers will live the experiences through, and then ultimately boil their experiences down to in memory. The design skills for this, as well as the Backwards Design process, are part of the ELVIS Toolkit in part 2 of the book.

As we help shape the kinds of stories our experiencers construct from their discomfort zone experiences, we must also ensure that they have the potential to significantly impact the special kind of narratives needed for *transformative* experiences—that is, our identity narratives. As the famous narrative researcher Joseph Campbell noted, the arc of the hero's external adventure was ultimately to bring about a change of consciousness of oneself, a new identity and with it a new way of being in the world. Now that we know a little bit more about humans as story animals, we need to build on this foundation of narrative psychology and learn more about identity as the final piece of the ELVIS Framework for designing transformative experiences.

# 4 ■ Identity Construction Deconstructed

How Our Sense of Self Drives Transformation

*I wanted only to live in accord with the promptings which came
from my true self. Why was that so very difficult?*

—Hermann Hesse,
*Demian*

*We're all just animals. That's all we are, and everything else is just an
elaborate justification of our instincts. That's where music comes
from. And romantic poetry. And bad novels.*

—Elvis Costello,
British musician

Identity impact is the third and final element of the ELVIS Framework (see figure 5). It refers to our dynamic and evergreen process of becoming. Who are you today? Who were you yesterday? Who do you aspire to be tomorrow? The answers to these questions are shaped by a combination of identity factors: our experiences, our

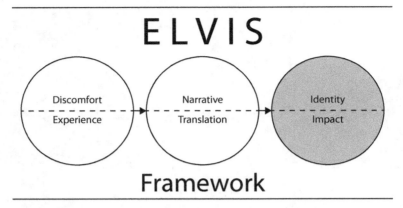

**Figure 5:** Experiential Learning Variables & Indicators System

biology, our culture, our relationships with others, and our private inner lives.

Since we have defined a transformative experience as a special kind of experience (one that changes who we are or who we want to become), the cognitive process by which we integrate these identity factors to forge our sense of self is an important tool for designers of transformative experiences. In fact, identity development is the keystone element of transformative experiences, connecting our discomfort zone encounters with narrative translation to produce experiences that can change our sense of self. Let's find out how identity construction and transformation works.

### Transformation Begins with the Identity You Have

In my 20s, I ran a school of martial arts for about 10 years. My founding partners and I trained hundreds of students over the years and refined a unique and highly experiential program that often broke with traditional martial arts instruction. For one thing, we did not use a one-size-fits-all curriculum but rather allowed students to chart their own pathways based on their abilities and preferences. I had one student, a tall, thin, and very shy man in his 40s named Seth, who worked particularly hard and almost never missed class. But he definitely went his own way, exploring many different aspects of styles we taught. Whenever it came time to move up in belt rank, Seth never belt-tested. He remained a white belt over the course of two years. And then one day he simply disappeared without explanation or even saying goodbye.

Many years after I had closed the school, I ran into Seth at a supermarket. He approached me and asked if I remembered him, falling into a karate stance to help jog my memory. After a laugh between us, he said he wanted me to know why he never tested and also why he left. Almost as if he had rehearsed this chance meeting in hopes it might happen, he explained to me that he was an adult survivor of child abuse, but that he had spent most of his adult years battling his identity as a *victim* of child abuse. His therapist had suggested that he take a martial arts class in order to confront his fears about personal vulnerability and helplessness—in other words, to bridge his identity from victim to survivor. That's when he came to my school. When he had accomplished his goal of finally changing his victim identity into a survivor-and-thriver identity, a stronger, more secure, and unafraid version of himself emerged. At that point, his training was complete.

Then, right there in the dairy aisle, he snapped to attention, bowed, thanked me, and was gone—again. I thought I had simply been teaching sidekicks, joint locks, and hip throws. Little did I know that he was having a transformative experience the whole time. The identity he walked in with was transformed into the newer and more powerful identity he walked out with. Seth never belt-tested because he was *always* testing himself from day one, and he earned his own personal black belt in identity growth as a result.

Seth's identity growth taught me that even when an experience is carefully designed (my methods of teaching martial arts were highly intentional and structured), there is always a shadow experience going on that cannot be designed, and sometimes is not even known. This shadow experience is made possible by what you design, but it is unique to each individual experiencer and depends wholly on the identity they have at the onset. It's like a tree of many branches. Your design may form the trunk that connects them all, but each branch is its own, producing its own leaves and stretching out to the sun in its own way. For any experience you design, there are as many shadow experiences going on as there are experiencers, all based on identity.

### Identity Theory 101: We Are All Identity-Fluid

At the very heart of the example of Seth the Survivor and the other stories throughout this book is the powerful influence of identity—who we think we are and who we want to become. The poet Walt Whitman summed it up nicely in 1867 when he asked

> *Oh me! Oh Life! of the questions of these recurring.*
> . . . . . . . . . . . . . . . . . . . . . . . . . . . . . . . . . . . .
> *. . . What good amid these, O me, O life?*
> *Answer.*
> *That you are here—that life exists and identity,*
> *That the powerful play goes on, and you may contribute a verse.*

In one elegant sweep, Whitman connects our struggle for identity with narrative and our experience of life as a story. Modern social identity theory posits that we each possess multiple identities comprising the psychological Self. We wear them like hats on different occasions: woman, man, gender fluid, older person, younger person, leader, parent, child, brother, sister, athlete, artist, and so on.

> We each possess multiple identities comprising the psychological Self. We wear them like hats on different occasions.

Each of our identities is an agent capable of action in the world (choices, behaviors, social connections, role taking, and more). Our identities often overlap or they may be arranged in dynamic hierarchies where one identity is dominant in certain situations but rather subdued in others. At times, our identities will harmonize with one another, making us feel good and in accord with the world and ourselves. At other times they conflict with one another or with identity standards and expectations that society holds for us, making us feel bad or in discord with the world and ourselves.

Identity traumas are a kind of transformative experience where our identities conflict with one another (sometimes drastically), demanding a reconstruction of the Self. In her boldly vulnerable book *Scarred* (San Francisco: Chronicle Press, 2019), Canadian actress Sarah Edmondson gives a gripping account of how her identity as an eight-year member of the NXIVM cult was intentionally put into conflict with her other, healthier identities, which were gradually hijacked or even entirely surrendered:

> *I would come to learn that while purporting to bond us closer as strong, evolved women, Keith [the cult leader] was undermining our relationships to each other in a harrowing, behind-the-scenes way and trying to eliminate the relationship each of us had with ourselves—for his own personal benefit.* (24–25)

Only after years of deprogramming therapy and a kind of self-reintegration healing process was she able to arrive at a new set of identities that, ironically, finally achieved what the cult had falsely promised her—to become a strong, self-actualized leader.

Michael Phelps, the most decorated Olympian in history, has made it his public mission to shine a spotlight on mental health and the tremendously difficult transformations that Olympic athletes must make as they forge new post-Olympics identities that can carry them into a new future.

The intense focus and single-mindedness needed for performance at the highest levels left his other identities undeveloped and uninhabited. After his Olympic career ended, he struggled to reinvent himself as a multidimensional person. Similar challenges are common among other former Olympians, for whom suicide rates average higher than for the same-aged populations when these identity challenges go unresolved.

In the excellent documentary film *The Weight of Gold* (Century City, CA: Searchlight Pictures, 2020), he remarks, "We're human beings. Nobody is perfect. . . . We all need to ask for help sometimes. . . .

We need somebody that can let us be ourselves and listen, allow us to become vulnerable, somebody who is not going to try and fix us."

These challenges ring true for both Olympians and everyone else facing major transitions in life. We see the same kind of identity resorting and reinventing in many disguises following identity traumas or identity conflicts: veterans returning from deployment and rejoining civilian life, survivors of catastrophic events who deal with life priority reshuffling and survivors' guilt, people who are facing chronic illness and those with life-altering injuries or surgeries, and ex-convicts after lengthy incarcerations as they strive to invent themselves anew and reengage in a most unwelcoming society.

> When life knocks us around, we are invited to abandon former ideas about who we are and dig into our undiscovered depths to conjure new identities that will carry us forward into the unknown.

We also see it in more ordinary situations, such as the identity changes that accompany illness, injury, divorce, the death of a spouse, or parents becoming empty nesters when their children have all flown. When life knocks us around, we are invited to abandon former ideas about who we are and dig into our undiscovered depths to rekindle and reharmonize old identities or conjure new ones that will carry us forward into the unknown.

In all cases, far from being fixed, our identities are fluid throughout our lives as we learn, grow, and age. The old adage proclaiming that "a leopard cannot change its spots" misses the point entirely. It would be far more accurate to say that it is not the leopard's spots that change, but the leopard itself that changes underneath the spots. In fact, the leopard cannot *not* change. Neither can we.

### Identity Types

> We all possess multiple identities. We are, each of us, a plurality.

We all possess multiple identities that simultaneously coexist within our sense of self. We are, each of us, a plurality. Identity is not monolithic. As I often say in my workshops, possessing multiple identities is not a disorder. It is the sign of a healthy, intricate, and adaptable sense of self. Importantly for designers of transformative experiences, identity theory recognizes three important identity types that we all inhabit:

**Role identities:** Describing the various roles and functions we perform in society, such as our professional identities (our jobs), being a student, a coach, a parent, and so on.

**Social identities:** Describing how we connect to others through group affiliation, such as gender, race/ethnicity, age, political party, religion, team membership, or even belonging to less formal groups like book clubs, being a sci-fi fan, or the huge social identity factor now dominating the world: social media.

**Personal identities:** Describing elements of our sense of self that set us apart from everyone else and articulating our unique way of living a life, of being in the world, and of inhabiting our own narratives. These are the deeper stories we share only with an intimate few or may tell only to ourselves about who we are. These are our secret identities, and they typically exist well below the surface, rooted within our subconscious.

Our various identities fall into one or more of these types, but they overlap. While it's all well and good to sort our identities into these clean categories, it's not how we live. Our sense of self is like a James Bond identity martini—shaken *not* stirred—with different ingredients blended thoroughly into an ever-changing whole.

But for designers of transformative experiences, these identity categories are indeed tremendously useful as a way to become more insightful and strategic about the different kinds of experiencers for whom we are designing and what kinds of identity challenges and changes they may experience within our designed discomfort zones. For example, we find a deepening of potential transformation with each identity type, starting with role identities and progressing to personal identities, where our most powerful transformations occur. Let's revisit these categories to see how.

### Role Identities as the Easiest and Most Frequent to Change

Every time we land a new job or take on a new position in our lives or the community, we experience a change of role identity. This will happen to us several dozen times in our lives. It is also quite expected and considered normal, making such changes easier for us psychologically. Many of the roles we will inhabit in our lives are well defined or even prescribed with off-the-shelf templates for what is demanded of us in those capacities. In other cases, the roles have more flexibility or even require us to invent them. Usually, it is a mix.

Some roles run much deeper, of course, such as being the leader of your organization, with hundreds or thousands of people depending on you and your ability to lead effectively, or becoming a parent, a role that morphs tremendously over time as our children age. Role identities also tend to get rearranged more frequently in our identity priority list. Being a son or a daughter may be the most important role we inhabit in our younger years, but it changes drastically in adolescence as our peer relationships rise, and again in adulthood as our independence grows. When our parents pass away, our role identities as their children persist for the rest of our lives, but the performance of those roles takes on a different form and meaning as we then become the elders in our families.

The same is true for leaders in all domains. As the role-identity torch for being the leader is passed into our hands, the influence of our past experiences as the protégés of our previous mentors entwines with our own aspirations for how we will be similar, different, and hopefully better. But for both our more shallow and deeper role identities, changes in this category are often easier and more frequent for us to navigate.

There is a hidden hazard with role identities—what I call the "talent trap." This is where we develop certain skills or aptitudes or proficiencies associated with the performance of one or more of our role identities, and then confuse those talents or competencies for who we are. This is related to the saying, "You are not your job." And yet, highly dedicated, passionate, and skilled professionals fall into this trap all the time, especially if they are very good at what they do. We all have encountered people caught in this snare, or may even have been ensnared ourselves from time to time.

In the talent trap, one's titles, the scale and scope of one's responsibilities, salaries, awards, and other badges and monikers of role identity status become the dominant form and measure of personal worth. All aspirations and goals are defined in terms of the realm of that role. A unidimensional identity emerges. When this happens, a person's professional identity overshadows all other elements of the Self, creating a kind of identity prison that confines the imagination from even considering what other potentialities exist. This again speaks to the challenges of Olympic and professional athletes struggling to reinvent themselves after their sporting careers are over, for example. It also includes any circumstance where someone sees a lot of early success and begins to identify only with the reputation connected with that success.

For corporate leaders designing transformative experiences for their employees, we can recognize the talent trap as a comfort zone. With people caught in the trap, one's role identity and the "ladder of success" associated with it in the corporate world is very attractive and well defined. In fact, a person's single-minded investment in a prominent role identity or job is often a conscious way of avoiding other areas of their lives, especially when prospects in those other areas are not going so well. Designing experiences that touch only a person's professional role identity may inadvertently reinforce this trap. The opportunity here is to go deeper.

For corporate leaders, role identity transformations are often the starting point of transformative experience design, but inviting the possibility of also delving into social and personal identity changes is essential. For those caught in the talent trap, this means inviting your experiencers to put themselves at risk by abandoning their competencies to explore discomfort zones in which those competencies are no longer valid—places where all we are left with is our incompetencies, the places where transformative experiences begin.

For more stories on the value of incompetencies for identity growth, visit this book's companion site at DesigningTransformative Experiences.com.

### Social Identities as a Deeper Pathway for Change

Social identities are closer to our hearts than role identities, although they are often connected. They include the people and groups most important to us and describe our interactions with them. Our social identities provide us with our sense of belonging as well as our senses of exclusion and isolation. Think of your own isolation during the COVID pandemic, when you were sequestered away from colleagues, friends, family, and even strangers. Consider how it taxed your emotional experience as holidays, birthdays, work milestones, and other life events came and went.

Or consider the tremendous and increasing power of social media, especially on younger people. This domain includes everything from simply belonging to transient group chats to maintaining several social identities (screen and user names, avatars, and online personas) and then accruing as many followers and subscribers on TikTok, YouTube, or Instagram as possible to become an "influencer." Social scientists and marketing professionals who study social network analysis are currently in their heyday.

Not only does social media provide a sense of belonging and validation (and income for influencers), but the user experience in the apps and the online interactions they mediate are designed to release dopamine (the neurotransmitter governing pleasure and addiction) in our brains. That instant high from having your post liked or a video going viral, or the satisfaction of having someone accept your connection request is tied to our pleasure centers. These social experiences are only a swipe away on our smartphones. It is no mystery why school and work have a hard time competing with social media for our attention and why we incorporate social media tools into school and work more and more. Social media can be a powerful narrative tool for your designed experiences. It is also a powerful identity narrative tool.

Beyond temporary dopamine highs, strong social bonds also bolster long-term health benefits such as lower stress, increased quality of life, confidence and feelings of well-being, lower blood pressure, and more. Conversely, the lack of a sense of belonging and social interaction is associated with feelings of stress and the increased production of cortisol (the primary stress hormone), symptoms of anxiety and depression, and poorer health in general. We are, after all, social primates who gain a sense of ourselves through our interactions with others.

In addition to our self-appraisals about who we are, we also form reflected self-appraisals, which is what we think others think about us. And much identity research has demonstrated that reflected self-appraisals are quite important in determining our self-assessments, self-esteem, and sense of belonging and in governing our behaviors in different social contexts.

But changing our social identities is usually not as easy as changing role identities. For one thing, we typically possess and inhabit fewer social identities, making the ones we have that much more important to us. They are also much more emotional in nature because they include our emotional connections to friends, family, colleagues, community, and even strangers we meet. These many relations to others combine to form our social status, which is directly tied to our sense of self-worth. Consequently, we feel our social identities to be much "closer to the vest" than role identities. In fact, our social identities are co-constructed through social dialogue and therefore are partially dependent on others to create and to change.

Parents raising children know this well, as they talk to their kids about who they are, how they behave (or don't), what they want in life, and who they want to be. Through this continual dialogue with parents, children gain a sense of self. And this identity conversation continues into adulthood as the parent-child relationship evolves as both grow older into the seasons of life.

A similar social identity co-construction occurs with coaches and athletes in the domains of motivation, self-actualization and goal setting, and physical/mental training programs. And of course, experience design leaders and their experiencers will engage in a version of this dialogue as well. The very nature of the mentor-protégé relationship is one of co-construction and co-narration of social identity that operates in both directions. In this way, mentors and protégés define each other.

The co-construction of social identities is a tremendously important aspect of designing transformative experiences. Our experiencers will need social bonding with both the experience leader/designer (you) and fellow experiencers. The social aspect of the group, cohort, or team sharing the experience can make or break an experience design as individual members of a group both have and narrate their discomfort zone experiences. In my work, I've dubbed this the "Social Cohort Effect," and it is often not sufficiently attended to by designers. We will discuss strategies for how to design with the cohort effect in mind in chapter 9.

### *Personal Identities: The Key to Unlocking Transformative Experiences*
Personal identities are where the deepest transformative experiences occur. We have even fewer of these identities. For some people, there is only one. This is the closest we come to a "core identity," and it is therefore highly treasured and carefully guarded, whether we like ourselves or not. Our personal identities are where we feel we live. We feel them to be our "truest" versions of ourselves.

Role identities and social identities are commonly felt to be performed and include a great deal of external expectations and identity standards, which we experience as pressure to behave in certain ways. Personal identities, however, are shaped more by internal desires and realizations, positive and negative. Our personal identities powerfully inform how we inhabit all our other identities. They also incorporate our many past personal identities, who we were at age 5, 10, 20, 30, and so on. These past selves are woven together in memory and coexist in our present to generate a legacy of identity in which we become our own ancestors, yielding a multidimensional and integrative current Self.

Further, it is our personal identities we feel to be the most constant over time, and perhaps that is true . . . until it's not. Until we experience a deeply rooted transformation. Until we grasp that we do indeed have our hands on the steering wheel of who we are, and decide to start driving. That is, to intentionally direct our experiences of ourselves within the unfolding of it all.

When that happens, we can develop an aptitude for transformative experiences that grows. Such experiences can then become more sought after, more possible for us, and more frequent. Transformations of personal identities activate our core values, worldviews, and deeply held beliefs about ourselves. Consequently, these changes have the most far-reaching ripple effects on our lives. And this is where designers of transformative experiences must go.

> A critical challenge for designers is to create opportunities for experiencers to activate and explore their own personal identities.

Therefore, a critical challenge for designers is to create opportunities for experiencers to explore their own personal identities within the context of the designed experience. This is done by creating the time, space, and context for such experiences; providing structures to support deeper experiences that engage those core values, worldviews, and beliefs about ourselves; and harnessing our innate meaning-making narrative skills (all covered in part 2 of this book).

In the most powerful transformative experiences, people find themselves grappling with their sense of self in order to understand who they are from an entirely new perspective, and ultimately taking more conscious control of their identity narratives as a result of the experience. In order to facilitate this process through the experiences we design, we need to better understand what identity narratives are and how they work.

## Identity Narratives: Our Most Prized Possessions

Not by any coincidence, narrative is the form our identities take, including role, social, and personal identities. Springing forth from our natural narratability to storify our lives, identity narratives contain the precious information of who we are in the world. And they are living, breathing, and changing narratives unique to each of us. Ask me who I am and I will tell you a story. Ask me at a family barbecue and you will get a very different story than if you asked me at a job interview. Ask me for those same stories in 10 years' time and they have each evolved. My "self-stories" and yours are based on our lived experiences. This includes a grand amalgam of our nature and our nurture, our physical and biological circumstances as human animals combined with our experiences and their resulting narratives, all nested within the larger social and cultural narratives of the societies and cultures within which we were brought up.

Psychologists Dan McAdams and Kate McLean describe narrative identities as "a person's internalized and evolving life story, integrating the reconstructed past and imagined future to provide life with some degree of unity and purpose" (D. P. McAdams and K. C. McLean, "Narrative Identity," *Current Directions in Psychological Science* 22, no. 3 (2013): 233–238, https://doi.org/10.1177/0963721413475622). Crucially, the very fact that they are malleable narratives provides the key mechanism by which transformative experiences result in changes to our sense of self, as we will see.

Our identity narratives first emerge as richly contextualized self-stories during adolescence, complete with roots in the past and projections into the future. Before adolescence, our stories about ourselves are more unidimensional in nature, centering on self-description. Ask a child under 10 you know about who they are. You'll likely get name, rank (age and grade level), and some traits they possess: interests they have, activities they like, people, food, games, movies or music they like or dislike. Simple, direct, innocent. Even if their early years have included tremendously important positive or negative experiences that will affect the rest of their lives, they have typically not yet begun to reflect on and integrate these kinds of experiences into a tightly cohesive and introspective self-story. Their "narrative capacity" has not yet arrived on their "identity scene," as it were.

Leaders who design transformative experiences for preadolescent kids, heads up! We cannot dump a highly structured and introspective exploration of narrative self on them and expect good results, or perhaps any results at all. Crickets would be more common. And in some cases, such an approach will backfire by disengaging and "losing" the audience for an otherwise very engaging experience. However, designers can and should lay the groundwork for a deepening of the narrative translation of an experience for preadolescent children. This can include basic questions that cause a child to begin to reflect on their internal states during experiences that are new to them or push their comfort zones. Try it.

Ask a child you know to recount one of their more recent favorite experiences. It will typically be centered on the external events. Then ask some simple self-narrative-inducing questions: What did you think about when you learned the details about this experience or activity? How did you feel during the experience? How do you feel now? How do you think the others around you felt? How do you describe this experience to others? A simple story centered on the self begins to take shape. Such questions can lead to an emerging understanding of how the experience affected them internally, and that is the direction we need to gradually introduce for younger kids. It is also an appetizer for where we need to go with adults.

During adolescence and into adulthood, our identity narratives expand to include both subjective and objective dimensions, also known as first-person narratives and third-person narratives. That is, we extend our ability to see ourselves both from behind our own eyes and from outside ourselves, as others might see us or as characters in a scene we are watching (theory of mind once again). New contexts emerge. We see ourselves as strangers and familiar at the same time. We begin to see how our past experiences have shaped our present and may govern our future choices and behaviors. We weave our evolving presence over time into a coherent and resilient identity arc. And this maturing of our self-perceptions tracks in lockstep with our developing narrative ability at the same ages.

We also begin to recognize multiple identities existing within us simultaneously: role identities, social identities, and personal identities. The identity "hats" I mentioned above begin to form as we become experimental "mad-hatters" and try various ones on for size.

They allow us to interact with the world and with others in an increasingly larger number of ways. To this we also add our many past selves, now coexisting in our present alongside our possible future selves, glimpsed through eyes of aspiration. The question "Who am I?" begins to take on many different and more sophisticated narrative answers.

With this increasing depth of identity, we see ourselves as living a complex drama—a narrative seeded with opposing forces and expectations from both external agents (peers, parents, teachers, bosses) and internal sources (our own personal standards, expectations, and aspirations). We begin to struggle with questions about existence and our place in the world. Through our adult years, the notion of being on a life journey through time and space, nested within a much larger and longer narrative of cosmic and spiritual proportions, grips our imagination and frames our experiences into a central narrative arc with a coherency of Self.

> Our identity narratives dynamically serve to explain us to ourselves.

Our identity narratives dynamically serve to explain us to ourselves. We form narratives for our various role identities and our social identities, and more intimate self-stories for our personal identities. Through them all, we create meaning in our lives and engage and interact with the world and others in it through a multitude of selves, each capable of different perspectives and different actions. And each one dynamic.

You can think of identity as similar to our bones. Bones seem solid and fixed and first glance, but on closer inspection we find them to be ever-changing tissues, remodeling themselves continually. And just like the osteoclast cells that constantly tear down our bones and the osteoblast cells that constantly rebuild them, so too our identities, as narratives, undergo constant reinvention and growth. As we've seen, sometimes this occurs almost imperceptibly slowly and other times swiftly through significant and life-altering experiences. But it is the fact that our identities take the form of narratives that gives us access to design transformative experiences and then author the resulting narratives that in turn shape who we are and who we want to become.

As ELVIS Experience Design Leaders, we must embrace this process of identity narration and provide opportunities for our experiencers to explore it. The capacity to consciously govern the process of the narrative translation of any and all of our experiences unlocks the deeper work of authoring our own identity narratives in more intentional ways. This is the essential aptitude for transformation and why we say that transformative experiences always ultimately come from within.

Before we fully develop these skills for constructing identity narratives from our experiences, we tend to feel that everything *happens to us*, beyond our control. We are somewhat like puppets being pushed around by the external world of other people, events, and forces. However, as we develop and actualize our self-narrative abilities, we begin to assume authorship of our lives and ourselves. Instead of feeling like puppets, we become engaged agents, capable of purposive action and change. Living becomes an act of artistic expression.

> As we actualize our self-narrative abilities, we assume authorship of our lives and ourselves. Living becomes an act of artistic expression.

But know this: the extent to which people develop robust skills for constructing such identity narratives, or even becoming fully aware of their own unconscious narrative identities, varies widely for different people and at different ages. Some people may never get there.

You may be dealing with kids who struggle with self-regulation and executive function. You might be in charge of teens who are all over the map for theory-of-mind acuity. Or you may be leading adults whose self-narrative abilities (conscious or unconscious) have not developed much beyond late adolescence. Many people simply never tap into their own resources for doing the kind of inner inquiry and reflection combined with the forms of outer expression necessary to intentionally assemble and modify their personal identity narratives. Some only do so during or after middle age, when a tidal sense of mortality and retrospection floods in—the "midlife crisis." Others, however, are jolted into it at various times through extraordinary experiences that hold the potential for personal transformation. That is, of course, where we designers come in, part Sherpa to guide the journey, and part Shaman to help deepen their meaning of Self.

## Ripple Effects of Transformation Are Unstoppable

Part of our role as ELVIS Experience Design Leaders is to embed our experiences with narrative-creating elements that equip and impel experiencers to author the narrative translations of their experiences in ways that tap into their identity narratives, particularly personal identity narratives. Practical design tools for doing this are included in the ELVIS Toolkit in part 2 of the book.

If we do this right, our experiencers not only assume experiential authorship but also reveal, activate, and then modify their existing identity narratives in the process. When this happens, we see ripple effects as their newfound sense of ownership of life events transfers from the domain of the experience we've designed into other domains of their lives. Like Tabitha the Traveler ending it with her boyfriend, quitting her job, and going back to school after her trip to Europe. Or Diane the Dragon Lady reshaping her professional reputation as an inclusive leader. Or Seth the Survivor rebuilding his sense of self through the martial arts to more fully inhabit his life without fear. Or me changing the nature of my work with Jane Goodall after one night with "just Jane." Once started, the ripple effects of transformation are unstoppable.

And indeed, very often a transformative experience that we have can trigger transformative experiences for those close to us. This happens in marriage and divorce all the time (my own included), where one partner's identity-changing experience necessitates a change in the other, thereby changing the nature of the relationship where it may grow and deepen, or perhaps diminish and disappear. A change in a child's identity as the child matures and becomes an adult transforms the relationship with the parent and how the parent sees herself. An athlete's or an executive's growth and transformation through success changes their coach's self-perceptions as they share in the success, or the many failures behind that success. Again, mentors and protégés in all domains define one another through the intersection of their identity narratives.

Finally, ripple effects from positive transformation experiences often include a propensity for more transformative experiences to be ushered into one's life. As mentioned earlier, an aptitude for transformation takes hold, whereby once we understand and can own how such powerful experiences work, they become more sought after, more possible for us, and more frequent. This has certainly been true of my life and the many extraordinary experiences it continues to hold.

> As part of skillful design, transformative experiences become the elixir for a self-reflective and more self-aware way of being in the world.

When examined as part of skillful design, transformative experiences become the elixir for a self-reflective and more self-aware way of being in the world. And this impacts everything from relationships to life events, navigating the highest highs and the lowest lows, and in forging a new dialogue with the unknown that exists both out there in the world beyond us and deep within us. This kind of ripple effect makes us more likely to see the transformative potential in life's experiences all around us every day.

We see these kinds of ripple effects from transformative experiences in almost all cases. In fact, if there are *no* ripple effects, it indicates that while we may have a truly remarkable or extraordinary experience before us, it is not a transformative one. Far-reaching ripple effects are evidence of the depth and durability of a transformative experience beyond changes in role and social identities alone. These kinds of experiences seep into all areas of our lives and persist precisely because of their impact on our personal identity narratives.

Identity construction occurs whether we attend to it or not, whether we are aware of it or not. It is a narrative process that germinates within our lived experiences and blooms with the meaning we will ultimately forge from these experiences in terms of changes to our sense of self. This psychology behind identity construction is central to designing transformative experiences for ourselves and others, providing incisive tools to deepen and make the experiences we design more personally relevant. By understanding and then harnessing the way we construct our identities, we gain the perspectives needed to create opportunities for our experiencers to engage quite consciously in this empowering process of introspection and self-determination. What more could leaders hope for?

Now that you've recast yourself as a leader in the role of experience designer, and now that you understand the basics of the Experiential Learning Variables & Indicators System Framework, it's time to apply what we've learned so far in part 1 with the specific and practical design strategies and ELVIS elements I present in part 2: the ELVIS Toolkit.

PART TWO

# THE ELVIS TOOLKIT

# 5 ■ Transformative Experience Design Strategies

*I was training to be an electrician. I suppose I got wired the wrong way round somewhere along the line.*

—Elvis Presley,
American musician

This chapter begins with a sequence of experience design strategies that I highly recommend and use frequently both in my client workshops and in my own experience designs. If you are new to experience design, they are an excellent way to get started. If you are a seasoned pro, the following may be familiar or even offer nice twists on what you already do:

Backwards Design
3 × 3 Nested Design
Framing and Priming
Emergence
ELVIS Design Matrix

The ELVIS Design Matrix is the biggie. It contains the heart and soul of the Experiential Learning Variables & Indicators System. It includes the seven elements my work has revealed to be critical across transformative experiences:

Risk
Control
Immersion
Social and emotional involvement
Intellectual challenge
Identity matters
Meaning making

In the chapters that follow, we will unpack these seven elements with detailed tools for how to apply them in your own ELVIS Experience Design Leadership. By combining the seven elements with the overall design strategies we will cover here, you will have a robust ELVIS Experience Design Toolkit that you can return to again and again for inspiration, innovation, and reference.

## Backwards Design

I begin all my experience designs with Backwards Design. A lot of people purport to use this strategy in various ways in their work, but there seems to be a wide range of interpretations about what it really means. Let's take a deeper look into what it is and the tremendous potential it has for empowering us as Experience Design Leaders using ELVIS.

Backwards Design is more than simply "beginning with the end in mind." It employs reverse engineering wherein you first define your desired outcomes and then work back from there to determine the design strategy to achieve them. This is the common understanding of Backwards Design, but in the context of designing transformative experiences for others, it takes on a significantly deeper and more specific meaning.

Whatever experiences we design, our audiences will ultimately transform those experiences into narratives, as we have seen. Depending on the type of resulting narrative our audiences generate, they may become inspired; be moved to action, motivated to new aspirations, brought to tears; or experience any number of other outcomes. But when that process goes even further to challenge and change the audience's existing personal identity narratives, we have a transformative experience on our hands.

Therefore, considering what kind of narrative we want our audiences to construct when it's all over is the ELVIS version of "beginning with the end in mind," or Backwards Design. This is very different from the way we normally operate, where life comes at us and we react. This strategy demands that we pro-act instead.

The producers and designers of the popular TV show *The Voice* understand this on some level. On its surface, the show is simply a singing competition decided by a panel of rock and country superstars. However, the formula is actually based entirely on identity narratives. In the very first segment, called the blind auditions, contestants have only 90 seconds to sing for the panelists, who can hear them but not see them. If selected, contestants advance to the next round; if not, they go home. Before this audition, the producers assemble a short video on each contestant, explaining their journey, what this opportunity means to them, and how they feel about the audition.

Typically, being on the show is a tremendous opportunity and risk they have decided to take. Whether the contestants are 15 years old or 50, this short profile is nothing short of an identity narrative that presents their sense of self (in part), the projection of possible selves they hope for if they win or lose, and the personal meaning of the moment. Then, over the course of weeks, the panelists tutor the contestants as they prepare for each successive competitive performance that may advance them to the final round or eliminate them. Win or lose, however, it is this work with such highly successful mentors in pursuit of their own dreams of "making it" in the music business that is the most valuable part of the experience. The show chronicles the resulting changes in their identity narratives, from dreamer to competitor to experienced performer, and in many cases, to professional musician.

So as designers of transformative experiences using the strategy of Backwards Design, we begin with two key questions about the end:

1. What kind of resulting narrative do I want my audiences to generate from this experience (knowing we can only guide this process and not dictate it)?
2. How will that narrative intersect with (or even modify) their existing identity narratives?'

From the answers, we reverse engineer the design. For each component (each risk invitation, each intellectual opportunity, each social element we include) we must ask, "How does this particular component support the ultimate outcomes, as described by the answers to our two key questions above?" If it does nothing to support those outcomes, we eliminate it from our experience design. If it does support the outcomes, we seek to refine and seamlessly integrate it into the holistic experience. This strategy serves as a continuous and guiding gut check for our ELVIS designs, especially if we must change things on the fly as situations change. More on that coming up.

## 3 × 3 Nested Design

The 3 × 3 Nested Design is the next step after Backwards Design. The 3 × 3 Nested Design allows us to clearly visualize how and where to apply the seven elements of the ELVIS Matrix covered in the following chapters. I developed this model specifically for transformative experience design, after decades of experience with many other leadership design frameworks. It is easy to understand and simple to use. It is a three-phase design using a three-act structure within each phase, anchored on a central experience (see figure 6). The three phases are as follows:

1. **Pre-experience:** Assembly of cohorts or teams (for group experiences), preparations for the experience to come,

learning the identities of the experiencers, inviting experiencers to participatory design (chapter 7), beginning the experiencers' personal narratives of the experience

2. **Experience:** The project, training, session, task, course, mission, competition, lesson, event, trip, or other experience

3. **Post-experience:** Conclusive actions, assessments, meaning making, further personal identity integration, narrative compilation, sharing, cohort disbanding

Each of these three phases, in turn, follows a three-act structure:

**Act 1:** The call to action or adventure for that phase, including context setting, foreshadowing events and challenges, and articulating expectations, goals, and responsibilities

**Act 2:** The rising and falling of experiences that compose the "plot" of that phase, populated with a sequence of events, challenges, and other tasks and occurrences

**Act 3:** The climactic peak followed by the denouement for that phase

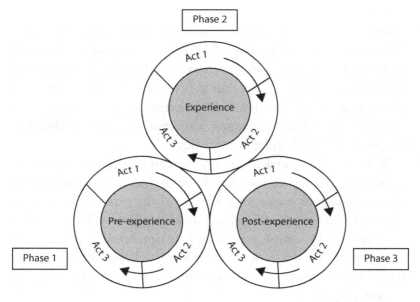

**Figure 6:** 3 × 3 Nested Design

Thinking about your experience design this way helps parse out how your experiencers will flow through what you have in store for them, much like a screenwriter plotting out the storyline for a movie and considering what the audience's needs are at any given point. Combining these phases, we can generate simple experience maps that help us plan, deliver, and change our ELVIS designs more easily. Further, each of the seven ELVIS Matrix design elements (explored below) can and should be applied to each of these three phases.

## Framing and Priming

Framing and priming are two powerful and relatively simple experience design strategies that I encourage all designers to become familiar with. They come into play as soon as interaction with your experiencers begins. You likely already know a lot about them (even if you don't know you do), because we experience both in our lives almost daily.

### Framing

Framing refers to the explicit precontextualizing of an experience. This is related to the "framing effect" in cognitive psychology, which describes how a person's choice from several different options is influenced more by how information is worded and presented rather than the actual information itself. But framing goes beyond this. I like to think of it as "managing your expectations," coupled with the power of "self-fulfilling prophecies."

What we think and feel going into an experience can greatly affect how that experience unfolds for us and how we interpret it. This includes our hopes for and fears of the experience, what we think will be risky or difficult, or what we think will be enjoyable and exciting. Of course, we might be surprised when things turn out very differently from what we expected, but more often we have a way of bringing about the outcomes that we mentally project and prepare for.

For example, my older brother Sean recently dropped his youngest child off at college, and I spoke to him later that night. As anyone who's had that experience can understand, he was a bit nostalgic and a little depressed at emptying the nest, the passing of a parenting era, and the end of childhood in his family (at least until grandkids come along). It was also a reminder of how old he himself has become. He was in grief. As we talked, he revealed that he had been dreading this day for some time, negatively anticipating how it might trigger him and wondering if he could handle it. He had framed the experience to be difficult, and it was.

As we talked, we began telling stories of our own flights from the nest when we were teens—how thrilling it had been to jump into a larger world of unknown and exciting possibilities. We also observed how lucky we had been to attend college at all, and how gratifying it was for him to now honor our parents' sacrifices by paying it forward to his own kids.

By the end of the chat, we had reframed the experience into a celebration of an important milestone. Reframing like that is a great tool, but framing ahead of time to shape an experience is even more powerful for experience designers. Not to say that some degree of grief wasn't warranted, but imagine how different the day would've been for Sean and his son if he had replaced dread with celebration from the start.

The ultimate meaning of any experience in our lives is powerfully shaped by the projected meanings we bring into it from the beginning. This makes framing a critical tool for preparing experiencers to create positive transformations for themselves within the experiences you design.

> The ultimate meaning of any experience in our lives is powerfully shaped by the projected meanings we bring into it from the beginning.

As we cover the seven ELVIS Matrix elements in the following chapters, I will present ways to explicitly frame and reframe how experiencers think about the opportunities you present to them, how they feel about it, what they hope to learn from it, and how you can guide those expectations.

The general techniques for framing include the following:

- The way you present the initial invitation or challenge of the experience (whether joining a team, a project, a competition, a new job, a class, an adventure, etc.)
- The kick-off meeting to set the tone or vibe for the social group and the individuals within it
- Frequent "pulse-check" discussion groups, reflections, and meaning-making opportunities along the way
- Various ways to facilitate individual identity growth through narrative translation of the experience

### Priming

Priming is a not-so-distant cousin of framing, but it is mostly unconscious. In cognitive psychology, priming refers to techniques that change our thought patterns and associations by tapping into how our brains and bodies process and access stored information. In its simplest terms, priming seeks to condition us for automatic associations between two stimuli. Exposure to an initial stimulus (the primer) alters our reaction to a subsequent stimulus (the target).

For example, my teenager sees a midnight blue Corvette in the parking lot (the kind of car he desperately wants to own). Later, at school he has to find a partner for science class and he chooses someone who is wearing a midnight blue shirt. He is probably not even aware of why he did that; it's unconscious. Now imagine using that same effect in a designed experience. In fact, this is something we experience almost every day. It is simple. And it is powerful.

The most common example is marketing. Advertisers build entire marketing campaigns on priming by associating their products with positive or provocative images, memorable taglines, and catchy music through targeted repetition. Priming is also used in cognitive therapy to help lower stress and reduce anxiety and depression. You might have experienced this yourself if you've had any therapy. Exposure therapy, kindness priming, and mitigation priming against bias and stereotyping are all forms of priming in cognitive psychology.

As ELVIS Experience Design Leaders, we can use it to prime our experiencers to associate our invitations to risk and discomfort with their own personal growth and transformation through positive messaging that links risk with possibilities for change. We can prime our experiencers to associate narrative translation with internalizing control, permission, and meaning making through examples and stories. And we can prime our experiencers to frame the opportunities we have created for them with identities that are bold, curious, and perseverant by signaling a spirit of adventure.

For more information on priming, visit the companion site for this book at DesigningTransformativeExperiences.com.

### Emergence

Despite our best-laid plans, unplanned things always occur. There is always an irreducible element of unpredictability in what happens during a designed experience and how it will impact experiencers. This is known as emergence, and although it is not a design strategy that we intend, we must be able to recognize it when it occurs and be ready for it.

Emergence is a word for ghosts in the design—the apparitions of unexpected, surprising, and undesigned parts of an experience—with unexpected ripple effects beyond. While we cannot plan for emergence, by definition, we can expect it.

> Emergence is a word for ghosts in the design—the apparitions of unexpected, surprising, and undesigned parts of an experience.

I used to fear emergence as an indicator that things have gone off the rails. Later I reluctantly accepted it simply as "shit happens" and resigned myself to dealing with it when it did. Now, however, I look forward to it as an indicator that the whole ELVIS is greater than the sum of its parts and that experiencers are finding personal relevance in the design.

When you as a leader combine the elements of ELVIS diligently, adapting your design from the experiencer's point of view, and the experiencers bring additional elements to the drama, the design takes on a life of its own in marvelous, if sometimes challenging, ways. I cannot think of a designed experience I have led that did not include emergence. In some cases, the emergent and undesigned components were the best and most important parts. But in all cases, emergence is an outcome of design; emergence cannot happen without it.

So, like ghosts in the design, emergence appears seemingly out of nowhere, affecting the experience in real time and often as ripple effects beyond the design. When emergence happens, we should be ready to recognize it and run with it. I will discuss specific emergence within several of the seven ELVIS Matrix elements.

**The ELVIS Design Matrix: "The ELVIS 7"**

Finally, we turn our attention to the heart and soul of practical transformative experience design: the ELVIS Design Matrix, or what I often call "the ELVIS 7" (see figure 7). As I mentioned above, there are seven elements: risk, control, immersion, social and emotional involvement, intellectual challenge, identity matters, and meaning making. They constitute the variables and indicators of the Experiential Learning Variables & Indicators System. Individually, each element represents an important design element for transformative experiences. But their real power is in concert with each other within each phase of an experience design.

Rather than thinking of the ELVIS 7 as a checklist of things to attend to or as a way to merely enhance what you are already doing as you design experiences (which it is quite good at, by the way), by now you can recognize the leadership paradigm shift that the ELVIS lens opens up. Used holistically, it is not simply a recipe or set of considerations to add to your work; it is an entirely new way to view your leadership.

Just as the king of rock and roll himself would strike that famous Elvis pose on stage, Experience Design Leadership through ELVIS is a stance we take as experience designers. It grounds us in a core philosophy that what we do as designers can and should have a

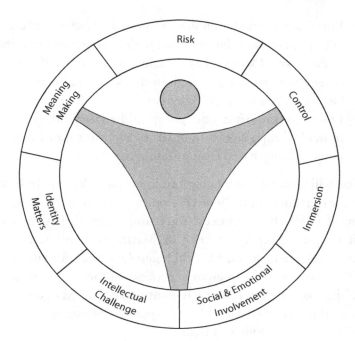

**Figure 7:** The ELVIS 7

powerful personal effect on our experiencers holistically, reaching them through multiple dimensions and on multiple levels. Importantly, ELVIS is not something we do *to our experiencers*;

> ELVIS represents an invitation to both the designer and the experiencer to cocreate a transformation.

rather, it is something we do *with them*. ELVIS represents an invitation to both the designer and the experiencer to cocreate a transformation.

Below are the ELVIS 7 presented in matrix format (see figure 8). In my work, I routinely use this ELVIS Matrix for a variety of purposes:

- I use it to examine not only entire experience designs but also their individual components, seeking the best mix of ELVIS elements for each activity, challenge, or risk invitation.

- I use it for evaluation in discussion with my experiencers, asking them to explore and rate their experiences using the elements of ELVIS as they are laid out here to see if my designs worked as I intended. In this way, it can serve to benchmark future ELVIS designs.
- I use it to consider my designs from the viewpoints of individual experiencers in order to determine how I might make identity-based customizations for them.

You will notice a 5-point continuum for each element, indicating that the elements can be "scored" along a range from less to more in terms of ELVIS best practices. You'll also notice that at the end of each chapter covering the ELVIS Matrix elements (chapters 6 through 12) I've included ELVIS Design Questions for you to consider and answer for any given experience element you are designing. The answer options for each question are ranked in order from 1 to 5. These correspond with the 5-point continuum seen in the ELVIS Matrix Overview in figure 8.

# ELVIS
Experiential Learning Variables & Indicators System

| 7 ELEMENTS OF TRANSFORMATIVE EXPERIENCES | ELVIS DESIGN CONTINUUM | | | | |
|---|---|---|---|---|---|
| Risk | 1 No Risk | 2 | 3 Moderate Risk | 4 | 5 High Risk |
| Control | 1 Leader Directed | 2 | 3 Equally Leader & Experiencer Directed | 4 | 5 Experiencer Directed |
| Immersion | 1 Low Immersion | 2 | 3 Moderate Immersion | 4 | 5 High Immersion |
| Social & Emotional Involvement | 1 Low Involvement | 2 | 3 Moderate Involvement | 4 | 5 High Involvement |
| Intellectual Challenge | 1 Leader Delivered | 2 | 3 Cofacilitated Leader + Experiencer | 4 | 5 Experiencer Driven |
| Identity Matters | 1 Low Identity Integration | 2 | 3 Moderate Identity Integration | 4 | 5 High Identity Integration |
| Meaning Making | 1 Unsupported or Unencouraged | 2 | 3 Supported & Semi-Structured | 4 | 5 Central & Extensive |

**Figure 8:** ELVIS Matrix Overview

But here I must emphasize an important point, and that is to consider this "scoring" scheme very lightly. To clarify, it does not directly measure anything. It is meant to characterize ELVIS elements in relative and subjective terms. In social science we would call it a self-referential rating scale. Or put another way, it is a quantitative system intended to be used qualitatively. The reason it works so well is because of the questions it is based on. To understand this better, let's take a close look at how the ELVIS Design Questions work.

The ELVIS Design Questions represent the "Indicators" part of the Experiential Learning Variables & Indicators System. You can use the design questions for each ELVIS Matrix element to examine an experience you are currently designing (or thinking about designing) or to examine an experience you have already designed, and can now look at through the ELVIS lens. In this way, the ELVIS Toolkit can be used *prescriptively* for your new designs or *descriptively* to assess and modify your existing designs, or both.

But our primary focus here will be using the tools of ELVIS as an intentional and personally tailored way to lead and to live out new experiences. For leaders, the ELVIS 7 and the design questions associated with each provide new insights for how you are currently creating experiences for those in your charge and how you can intentionally design experiences that have the potential to be transformative, both for individuals and for teams or organizations.

This matrix allows you to locate your design on the ELVIS landscape, from 1 (entry level) to 5 (representing a fully developed transformative design) (see figure 9). The questions and answer options themselves contain information that suggests how you might "level up" within each element to create more powerful experiences.

Let's put the ELVIS 7 to work with an example. Pretend I have designed an experience component where my participants must give a public talk and I want to look at risk (the very first element of the ELVIS Matrix). If I add up all my answers to the ELVIS Design Questions for risk about that component (the public talk), with each question contributing a score from 1 to 5, this gives me a total "score" for risk. I may get an average score of 4 (maybe less, maybe more), indicating my ELVIS Zone for risk for the public speaking component.

Then, I continue on down the ELVIS Design Matrix and "score" my public speaking component for each ELVIS element: control, immersion, social and emotional involvement, and so on. After I fill in the entire matrix, I can see in one snapshot how that experience component looks for each ELVIS element—the ELVIS Design Snapshot (represented in the histogram shown in figure 9).

This would represent my design intentions overall. I can use this to modify my experience designs more to my liking or customize them for individual experiencers. I can also add up all the scores for all the ELVIS Matrix elements together and generate an overall ELVIS score for any experience component and compare with other experience components. Finally, I can also apply the ELVIS Matrix to the three different design phases of an experience according to my 3 × 3 Nested Design (pre-experience, experience, and post-experience phases). Visit the companion site for this book for an automated ELVIS Design Matrix app that will produce ELVIS

# ELVIS
### Experiential Learning Variables & Indicators System

| 7 ELEMENTS OF TRANSFORMATIVE EXPERIENCES | ELVIS DESIGN CONTINUUM | | | | |
|---|---|---|---|---|---|
| | 1 | 2 | 3 | 4 | 5 |
| Risk | | | | ○ | |
| Control | | | | | ○ |
| Immersion | | ○ | | | |
| Social & Emotional Involvement | | | ○ | | |
| Intellectual Challenge | | | | | ○ |
| Identity Matters | | ○ | | | |
| Meaning Making | | | ○ | | |

**Figure 9:** ELVIS Design Matrix Snapshot Example for Public Speaking Component

"scores" and Design Snapshots for you based on your answers: DesigningTransformativeExperiences.com.

What this slicing and dicing of an experience design with the ELVIS Matrix does is to both zoom in and zoom out on a design to ensure I am hitting all the notes ELVIS has prepared for me. I can also do this qualitatively, without focusing on the numbers or scoring so much. For my own ELVIS designs, I typically use the scoring scheme for the most important components of an experience and use the matrix more qualitatively for the other components. The versatile use of the ELVIS Design Matrix, applied in different ways, helps designers examine their experience designs from different perspectives and use the seven elements holistically.

Finally, consider your audience. Experiencers have different needs. The "highest" possible answers to the design questions or the "highest" ELVIS Zones for your design may not be an appropriate objective—sometimes less *is* more. That is to say, it is not always the best practice to simply push each ELVIS element in your designs to the maximum level (5) of the matrix. It all depends on your audience, their identities going in, and your design goals. There is a practiced art in the application of ELVIS, just as there is an art to knowing your audience in the ways needed for ELVIS to be successful.

I treat the ELVIS Matrix like a stereo equalizer: the design is the music, the experiencer is the listener, and the combination of the two is the experience itself. For most music, if you push all the levels (hi range to bass) all the way up, the experience of listening to the music is horrible. Skillfully adjusting the levels makes all the difference. It may even be different for different people (customization). Sometimes, I invite those people to help make the settings just right for them (participatory design). It is very often the case that incrementally moving toward higher ELVIS Zones *during* your designed experience over time is the best strategy.

The ELVIS Toolkit is just that, a set of tools. It is not a formula. Use it to apply what you learn in this book in both strategic and tactical ways to enhance your skill in designing transformative experiences.

Like any tool, how *best* to use it is up to you. Remember, it won't be perfect right away. Your skills for applying ELVIS will grow over time as you become accustomed to viewing your leadership challenges through this lens and as you gain real-world experience using ELVIS with your protégés. That's why using this book as a design reference is so important as you begin to use ELVIS.

---

### Designer Tip

*The Design Sequence*

The ELVIS design strategies work best when they work together. For example, I always begin with **Backwards Design**, asking what kind of narratives I want my experiencers to take away with them at the end. Then I reverse engineer the experience using 3 × 3 **Nested Design**. When I launch into the three phases of the experience, I strategically use **Framing and Priming** all along the way to help guide the kind of narratives they are constructing from the experience. At each step I am looking for **Emergence** and ways that I can alter my ELVIS designs or invite others to help do so as well. Finally, I use the **ELVIS Design Matrix** and the tools found in the upcoming chapters to ensure every part of my design utilizes the research for what makes transformative experiences work.

---

# 6 ■ Risk

Strategies Using Risk's Many Disguises
and Hidden Transformative Powers

*Defeat, my Defeat, my deathless courage,*
*You and I shall laugh together with the storm,*
*And together we shall dig graves for all that die in us,*
*And we shall stand in the sun with a will,*
*And we shall be dangerous.*

—Kahlil Gibran,
"Defeat"

*Opportunities to find deeper powers within ourselves come when life*
*seems most challenging.*

—Joseph Campbell

Risk is at the very top of the ELVIS 7 because it is the most powerful and essential tool we have for designing transformative experiences (see figure 10). It is the main ingredient (but not the only one)

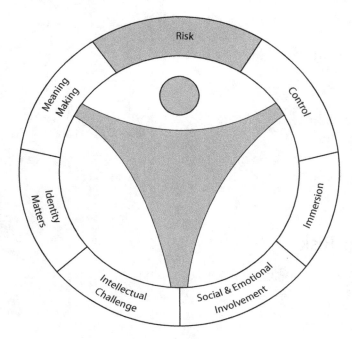

**Figure 10:** Risk

for the first component of the ELVIS Framework from part 1 of the book: discomfort zone experiences.

As we discovered in chapter 2, risk exists along a continuum from reckless to strategic and wears many disguises. Our perceptions of risk describe our discomfort zones. And although different people perceive risk differently, in all cases it is inversely related to our sense of agency. Therefore, a main task for designers is to present invitations for experiencers to enter their personal discomfort zones. That is, to give them opportunities to make *risk decisions* in areas where their sense of agency is low.

Recall also that risk comes in different flavors—physical, emotional, intellectual, and social—indicating that a large range of risk perceptions are in play in any given situation, which is a good thing from a design point of view. And so designing *risk decisions* into an experience requires us to first know something about our experiencers' identities and associated risk perceptions going in so that we can tailor our risk invitations to their personal discomfort zones. Therefore, this element works in tandem with the "identity matters" ELVIS element (coming up) and its tools for revealing experiencer identity narratives.

In this chapter, we will look at different examples and methods of designing and presenting risk invitations that demand risk decisions. At the conclusion of this chapter (and each chapter here in part 2), I present several design questions related to this ELVIS element.

### This Is Your Brain on Risk

To briefly recap from chapter 2, there are four important kinds of risk that appear in nearly every transformative experience:

- Physical risk: These are situations that put our bodies in harm's way and include uncertainty that we will emerge whole and healthy. Physical risks also present opportunities to increase our physical capacities and have new sensory and kinesthetic experiences.
- Emotional risk: These are situations that put our hearts on the line. They expose us to emotional and spiritual uncertainty and make us vulnerable. They also present opportunities for us to experience empathy, compassion, and spiritual insight in ourselves and others.
- Intellectual risk: These situations challenge our strategic and rational minds, including problem solving that requires our knowledge, creativity, and capacity to assess, learn and adapt.
- Social risk: Social risks make us vulnerable to losing our healthy connections and/or building unhealthy ones. Social risks also present us with opportunities to forge new positive attachments to others, raise our standing in social circles, and have new social experiences.

In discomfort zone experiences, these different types of risk are mashed together in the minds of experiencers. As I mentioned earlier, it is *perceived* risk in these areas that matters most. The higher the perceived risk in any area, the greater the perceived challenge, the lower the sense of agency that we can succeed, and the deeper we go into our discomfort zones. So, to be effective designers of discomfort zone experiences, we need a working knowledge of how people perceive and act on risk (or don't). A very practical place to start is how we often misjudge risk.

### How Our Perceptions of Risk Are Biased and Distorted

First off, in general as you've likely noticed, we don't "do risk" very well in our culture. Certainly in organizations we don't typically get rewarded for taking risks. Companies don't tolerate failure very well; in fact, they spend a lot of money assessing risk and avoiding it. Schools punish or even terminate teachers whose students don't score well on tests, despite overwhelming evidence that "teaching to the test" is bad for learning. Athletic directors and coaches face enormous pressure to win, not to take chances on new approaches that may result in losing, even in the face of evidence that the learning curves associated with new strategies often include losses at first. And what parent wants to see their child attempt something risky when the chances of failure are "too high," despite strong evidence that we stand to learn and grow more from failures than from successes?

Part of the reason we don't "do risk" very well in our culture is that we don't teach the skills of risk recognition, risk assessment, and risk decision-making, nor do we teach how to risk and fail and risk again in order to learn and grow. We are largely ignorant of the differences between intentional, strategic risks and reckless, cavalier risks or even the invisible risks all around us every day. And yet, we swim in a sea of risks all the time, from car rides to heartbreak to job loss to illness to death, and more. To live at all is to risk dying; they go hand in hand. It's about time we start getting good at risk, especially as experience designers.

> To live at all is to risk dying; they go hand in hand. It's about time we start getting good at risk.

But even when we do decide to pay attention to risk in order to make better risk decisions, we are subject to a number of cognitive and emotional biases that cause our perceptions of risk to be distorted. These biases reinforce a risk-averse approach to leading and living that is all too common in our culture. Knowing what some of these biases are is essential reading for designers of transformative experiences because both our protégés and we ourselves may unconsciously fall victim to them if we are not aware of them. And if we are aware of them, we can often use them to make our experiences better.

### Negative Outcome Bias

We often automatically associate risk with negative outcomes. Risk presents the chance of something bad happening, of course. But rarely do we flip the script and think of risk as the potential for something good to happen. In truth, it is both. We struggle to believe positive correlations exist between risks and benefits even when clearly articulated or statistically proven. For example, leaving a secure job in hopes of finding a better one, or embarking on a physically demanding exercise program after heart surgery, or even learning how to swim as an adult who is afraid of water are risks that have probable upsides. Yet people still tend to only see or disproportionately weight negative outcomes over potential positive ones. This leads to what researchers have called "pessimistic outcome appraisals." We then tend to perceive most risks as unacceptably high.

---

**Designer Tip**

*Recognize the Upside*

We need to expect a high level of negative outcome biases among our experiencers and be ready to help them recognize upsides to our risk invitations. Well-designed discomfort zone experiences include a tension between upside and downside risk perceptions. We will cover specific design strategies to do this, including framing and priming, in chapter 13, "The Holistic ELVIS."

*Emotion Association Bias*

Our emotions have a powerful influence on our perceptions of risk. Some researchers claim it is the dominant factor in our personal risk assessments. While it is not surprising that negative emotions lead to more pessimistic interpretations of risk and that positive emotions lead to more optimistic interpretations, what is surprising is how strongly mood can affect these appraisals. In fact, several findings show that as situations become increasingly complex, unanticipated, or stressful (indicators of discomfort), our responses are increasingly likely to be based on our emotions, just when logic could be needed the most in order to sort through such complexities.

---

### Designer Tip

*"Mood Up" Your Designs*

We should expect a wide range of emotional states among our participants, which therefore lead to a wide range of pessimistic to optimistic risk assessments for any given discomfort zone experience we design. Designers should seek design elements that "mood up," promoting positive emotions and positive reinforcement motivational techniques over negative ones.

---

*The Dread Factor*

Psychologists have long known that anxiety amplifies both the number and the intensity of our risk perceptions. Elements that increase our feelings of dread in the face of uncertainty include the risk being involuntary, being uncontrollable, and having potentially catastrophic outcomes. This helps explain why people tend to fear very low probability events such as airplane crashes and shark attacks more than far higher probability events such as car accidents and heart attacks. Additionally, both a person who has simply had a bad day and a person who is clinically depressed or anxious all the time are predisposed to interpret risks negatively. If they do decide to take a risk, they are likely to experience higher levels of stress because of it, even when the potential upsides outweigh the downsides.

> **Designer Tip**
>
> *Face Dread with Agency*
>
> We need to be able to recognize dread leading up to risk decisions and even possibly growing after an experiencer decides to take a risk. To some extent, fear and dread are essential elements of any discomfort zone experience. But we know from the research that the risk invitations we make to people should be voluntary, include options and multiple controls for the experiencer (agency), and ensure reasonable safeties in order to be effective.

*Status Quo Bias*

Change takes effort. So, too, does resisting change. And yet we often perceive change as "doing something" and resisting change as "doing nothing." We also tend to want to avoid unknowns. In decision theory this is called "ambiguity aversion," or more commonly stated as preferring "the devil you know over the devil you don't." In other words, we often prefer known risks over unknown risks even when the latter has potential for greater benefits. The problem is that we are not very good at assessing such probabilities. We often prefer to simply keep things the way they are. The net effect is a status quo bias that reinforces risk aversion even when the status quo is the riskier choice, such as with climate change or pandemic responses.

> **Designer Tip**
>
> *Design for Inquiry, Adventure, and Change*
>
> We need strategies that help people reveal and confront their status quo biases in order to embrace the unknown. In many cases, examining the risk by asking "How much will I regret *not* taking this chance?" can be an effective counter to status quo bias. Again, framing and priming (chapter 13) are powerful tools for this, as is the construction of an experience narrative that positions the experiencer to embody a spirit of inquiry and adventure (explored in chapter 3, on narrative, and chapter 12, on meaning making).

*Immediacy Bias*

Our bodies and brains have evolved to spot danger in order to survive. But not all danger. We are much better at recognizing risks when they are imminent. Such clear and present dangers have long included things like the violent attacks of animals or other people, fires, falling from great heights, storms, and any number of other immediate and urgent threats. Our senses are tuned to detect these kinds of risks. Our conscious and unconscious minds are quick to respond to them. But we are not very good at recognizing slow-moving, long-term, creeping threats like climate change, population overgrowth, economic collapse, or even pandemics that begin as strange infections in faraway places. The way we perceive risks is influenced by the timing associated with them. It's the immediate ones that we more quickly see, best understand, and experience most powerfully, whether that is warranted or not.

---

**Designer Tip**

*Add Immediacy to Your Risk Invitations*

Our risk invitations need to include some form of immediacy. This may look very different for the different kinds of risk involved in discomfort zone experiences: physical, emotional, intellectual, and social. But in all cases, the timeline for the initial risk experience needs to be short within the design, with a clear risk decision to kick it off, even if the deeper and more durable risk elements will unfold over a longer time frame.

---

*Groupthink Bias*

Most of us have experienced groupthink, and usually with hefty doses of frustration and decision paralysis added in as extra spices. Groupthink is related to peer pressure. It occurs when the desire for social harmony, or at least conflict avoidance, takes undue priority and leads to poor thinking and either bad decisions or no decisions. Family gatherings over the holidays are the classic example, but we also see it during work team meetings, group travel, team sports, and even in marriages. A workplace example is feeling obligated to back your boss's strategy out of loyalty even when you know it's the wrong choice.

But by succumbing to groupthink, we sacrifice our independent thinking, our creativity, and our contributions to innovation. Groupthink also drives in-group and out-group dynamics, challenging our efforts toward greater diversity and inclusion of people who are different from the majority or offer alternative voices and views. In terms of risk, groupthink can severely limit our capacity to recognize and respond to risks, depending on the prevailing views of the group.

---

**Designer Tip**

*Use Groupthink to Shape Experiences*

We need to recognize groupthink in both its positive and negative manifestations. In many cases, the pressures of groupthink are not visible without talking to individual experiencers in the midst of an experience. Sometimes they are invisible to the experiencers themselves. In my work, I often use embedded discovery group discussions to help reveal and then shape group dynamics at key points during an experience in order to bring unconscious elements of a discomfort zone experience up to a conscious level. The social cohort of an experience can be a positive design element if you plan for it to be so. This strategy and others like it are explored in chapter 3, on narrative, and chapter 9, on social and emotional involvement.

---

### Anchoring Bias

Anchoring occurs unconsciously, and it occurs everywhere. In risk perception in particular, it causes us to anchor our interpretation of a risk on the first information we get, simply because it's first. We then filter all subsequent information we get through the lens of our first impression, distorting our perceptions of the risk. For example, if I tell you, "We are going to do something terrifying today; we are going to skydive," you are more likely to view the skydiving as scary than if I said "We are going to do something exhilarating today." If you tell me that we need to have a difficult conversation about something personal, it is likely to be harder simply because you've set that expectation or anchored my perceptions on difficulty. We can impose anchors, or they can be imposed by others.

> ## Designer Tip
>
> ### *Make the First Anchor Work for You*
>
> First impressions of a risk are tremendously influential. Once set, they are hard to change. Any modifications to that first impression are likely to be small. This is known as "anchor and adjust," and research has shown that our adjustments from initial anchors are usually much too small to allow an accurate perception of a risk or prediction of an outcome. Therefore, our ELVIS designs must carefully consider how risk invitations are contextualized within the larger discomfort zone experience so that this natural tendency of anchoring works in service of a positive experience and not against it. Here again, individual differences in what people think is personally risky for them will play a large role in how they anchor.

## Values Bias

Values bias refers to our tendency to perceive risks in relation to our cultural and personal values systems, morals, and worldviews. That is, we interpret and form appraisals about risk in order to confirm or match our values. The Cultural Cognition project out of Yale University conducted a national survey, finding that cultural worldviews predicted people's perceptions of risks better than any other characteristic, including their gender, race, income, education level, personality type, or political affiliations (Dan M. Kahan, Hank Jenkins-Smith, and Donald Braman, "Cultural Cognition of Scientific Consensus," *Journal of Risk Research* 14, no. 2 [2011]: 147–174, DOI: 10.1080/13669877.2010.511246). People tend to dismiss or discredit information that is inconsistent with their beliefs and values while adhering to information that reinforces their beliefs and values. This is similar to "cherry picking" or what psychologists call "confirmation bias." Further, researchers have also shown that people are more persuaded by experts who share their value systems than those who do not, regardless of the quality of evidence those experts present. This helps explain why we see passionate disagreements and polarization across a whole range of topics these days.

---

**Designer Tip**

*Seek to Understand Experiencer Identity at the Start*

One size does not fit all. In order to design effective discomfort zone opportunities for different experiencers to take personally relevant risks, or even to perceive such opportunities as risky, we first need to gain an understanding of their values and worldviews (that is, their identities). The identities of our experiencers at the start are central to the nature of the experience they will have and the transformations of identity they may undergo. It is essential that we take the time to do this as early as possible in our designs. We explore identity and ways to include it in design more deeply in chapters 4 and 11.

---

*Risk Affirmation Bias*

Finally, experience designers have a risk bias that I need to point out. This is the tendency for designers of transformative experiences to think that what they themselves perceive as risky will also be perceived in the same way by their experiencers. While it is indeed essential to have designed transformative experiences for yourself in order to be effective in doing so for others, it is a mistake to assume that the same risks you experienced will work in the same ways for others.

---

**Designer Tip**

*See the Design through Your Experiencers' Eyes*

Our risk cognition biases point to a need for designers to focus on the subjective perspective of our experiencers rather than the content alone—that is, focusing on the ELVIS Framework and Toolkit elements from the *experiencer's personal point of view* to a greater extent than your own perception or the particular details of the risks and events in the design. In designed experiences that I have run for years, I am constantly tweaking the specific events, sequence, timing, and content in order to best adapt the ELVIS elements to the particular people in each given group. No two participants see risk the same way; therefore, no two experience designs should be exactly the same.

From a designer's point of view, the extent to which any given person might be affected by one or more of these risk biases can help us tailor our experience designs to their personal discomfort zones in terms of risks. So be on the lookout for these responses when you make a risk invitation and consider the designer tips for each one. It's very much like tailoring clothing so that it fits just right. Next, let's look at some specific tailoring tools and examples that can help us do this.

## Individual Risk Profiles and Risk Calculus

I used to assess experiencer risk perceptions much less formally, almost entirely intuitively. I thought I could get enough of a general sense for a group's risk comfort to adjust my experience designs accordingly, until one particular trip to Hawaii. I was studying a group of educators on a science learning journey that was part of their graduate work. Along the way were many opportunities for different kinds of risks, including night diving with manta rays in the open ocean, exploring deep and dark lava tubes and active volcanic sites, making science presentations to their peers, sharing personal stories of challenges they were facing in their personal lives, and more.

Among the group I worked with was a young teacher who had experienced a death in her family only days earlier and was experiencing Hawaii through the eyes of grief. There was a teacher on the cusp of retirement who had spent the past 15 years caring for her ailing husband and had not traveled at all for more than a decade. There was a middle-aged teacher trying not to quit the profession she had grown disillusioned with and was seeking to rediscover her passion. There was a childhood cancer survivor who had never given himself permission to adventure out in the world until now. There was a teacher who had just lost custody of her seven-year-old son in a bitter divorce and was trying to find a reason to carry on and be the mother her son could be proud of.

In short, there was not one monolithic group on one trip. There were 15 different experiences going on with 15 different risk lenses.

For me, not to go beyond the surface design and understand more about how each person might be living this experience was to be totally in the dark about what was truly happening. Although we strive to begin with the end in mind, the prearranged curriculum or planned design is only the beginning, not the ending point. Or as Morpheus famously says in the film *The Matrix*, "There is a difference between knowing the path and walking the path."

Sometimes, experience designs demand that we make some assumptions about the risk perceptions of our experiencers as a like-minded group. This is the case with "fixed" or "one-way" experiences such as designing rides at Disney or making a movie or writing a book. But for other experiences where there is two-way interaction, the power of understanding individual risk perceptions is key for designers. These include corporate teams, coaching, education, parenting, travel, and more.

In my workshops I cover how to build detailed risk profiles for individual experiencers, borrowing from two fields: decision theory and risk management. Both characterize individuals' risk perceptions with three descriptors:

- Risk attitude: Where one might be risk averse, risk neutral, or risk seeking
- Risk appetite: How much perceived risk a person will accept or wants
- Risk tolerance: How much deviation from their risk appetite a person can manage

For the detailed process, visit the companion site for this book at DesigningTransformativeExperiences.com. You can get a pretty good handle on it from asking a few simple questions and inviting experiencers to tell their stories of risk:

- What kinds of things come to mind when you think about risks?
- How would you describe your attitude toward different kinds of risky situations?

- What have been some of your best and worst risk experiences?
- Describe a time when you experienced too much risk and how you handled it.
- From 1 (low) to 5 (high), how would you rate your risk appetite for physical risks? For emotional risks? For intellectual risks? For social risks?
- Describe a time you have encouraged someone else to take a chance on something. How did you do it? How did it work out?

After risk profiles, we get to the specific risk calculus that people will do when presented with a risk invitation, which is largely unconscious. An important design practice is to raise this process to a conscious level in order to help experiencers recognize and respond to risk invitations in ways they intentionally choose. A relatively simple way to do this is through three questions that decision theory experts call the risk triplet:

1. "What can happen if I take this risk?" This question will typically skew negative initially to become "What's the worst that can happen?"
2. "How likely is that outcome?" This question is about estimating risk levels, which we are not very good at, as we discussed earlier.
3. "What are the consequences if that outcome occurs?" This question also typically skews negative.

Skewing negative at first is not necessarily a bad way to go, as considering worst-case scenarios places safety (physical or psychological) front and center. The problem arises when experiencers take it to negative extremes and stop there. Then it can become a paralyzing habit of catastrophic thinking, keeping us from taking any risks at all. But by including these questions explicitly in our risk invitations, we cannot only help experiencers to more consciously respond to risks, but we also gain the opportunity to frame the risk in more positive terms.

> **Designer Tip**
>
> *Reframe Risk*
>
> Help experiencers reframe the risk triplet calculus. The question "What can happen if I take this risk?" can be modified to "What positive things can happen if I take this risk?" Likewise, "How likely is that positive outcome?" "What are the potential positive consequences?" When we reframe the risk, we liberate ourselves from catastrophic thinking and allow ourselves and our experiencers to more consciously perform the next step in risk calculus—cost-benefit analysis, also known as "risk reward"—and to do it in a more balanced way.

In my work specific to transformative experiences, there is a fascinating kicker I've observed in terms of personal risk calculus. It very often turns out that the *risk outcome* (what finally results when someone takes a chance) is frequently not as important as the *risk decision* itself in the end. In other words, simply deciding to take a chance on something within one of your discomfort zones is central to having a transformative experience and often represents the highest hurdle of the experience. The actual result of that decision is quite commonly of secondary importance, good or bad. For example, let me take you back to Africa and a woman named Sally.

We were trekking up the Ngare Sero River gorge near Lake Natron in the East African Rift Valley. I was leading a group of about 20 along with local guides. We were headed to a beautiful waterfall at the high origin of the gorge. As we made our way, the rocky sides of the gorge grew steeper and the walking ledges narrowed. Sally seemed nervous, and I assumed it was due to the moderate heights and the rushing water below. It was not. She was nervous about contracting schistosomiasis, a disease caused by a parasitic flatworm that sometimes lives in warm and shallow bodies of water in Africa and other places. Although not lethal, the parasite can enter the body through the skin and cause intestinal problems if not treated. It is certainly something to be avoided. However, it is not typically found in cold rushing water far away from human civilization and had not been recorded in this area or on this particular river.

As we had to get in the water and cross the river several times on the way, I discussed these facts with Sally before our first crossing. We also discussed the recourse of simply opting out of this particular risk. She decided to trek on, eventually reaching the falls and even deciding to swim under and through the waterfall into the cave-like tunnel beyond. It was quite a place—a somewhat secret and magical oasis of dappled sunlight, swaying palms, a rocky cave, and cool, flowing water. Noticing her obvious delight and joy at this moment as she frolicked and laughed with the others, I made sure to ask her about it in an interview many months later.

To my astonishment, she told me that more than any other experience she had in Africa (including climbing Kili, working in African schools, seeing the Serengeti, visiting AIDS orphanages, and more), the waterfall moment was her highlight. But it was not the simple pleasure of experiencing the falls at the end of the journey; it was instead the moment she made the risk decision to step into the water at that first river crossing and the pride of accomplishment that came with it. Calculating the risk of parasites and her discomfort zone because of it, against other factors that indicated it was indeed safe, and then deciding to take that chance and deal with the consequences whatever they turned out to be, was a moment where Sally felt a sense of control and ownership over her experience. I later learned that this was an element lacking in Sally's life in general. She had been feeling pushed around by life lately, fostering a sense of passivity on her part. "Until that moment," she said, "I'd been feeling like a passenger on the plane. But when I decided to take that chance early on in the trip, I became the pilot. I still am." Her river moment was her transformative experience, prompting her to make big changes in life back home, including quitting a job she disliked, applying to several doctorate programs, and asking her girlfriend to marry her. She decided to own her life again.

I did not predict that Sally's largest risk would be crossing a stream. I had not designed this part of the experience with much risk in mind. I certainly did not "design" the stream crossing. It was simply part of the hike to the falls. I was focusing on larger, more obvious risks like crossing the Serengeti and climbing Kilimanjaro. But I was younger and earlier on in my experience designing and so unknowingly suffered from risk affirmation bias—mistakenly assuming that what I thought was risky would be the same for others. In this case it worked in reverse. I did *not* think crossing the stream would be considered risky for anyone. But had I included a participant risk profile approach in my design and had more discussions about perceived risks with the group, I would've better understood or perhaps even predicted this risk decision for Sally. As it happened, we dealt with it in real time, and it turned out to be a keystone experience for her. And I learned the central importance of risk decisions and risk invitations in the process.

It's a phenomenon I've now seen over and over in my work. The take-home lesson for designers is that we must ask ourselves some simple questions in the design process:

- What are the risk invitations in my design, and how am I making them?
- How are these interpreted as risk decisions for each person in this experience?
- What do their risk profiles tell me about how they might respond?

---

**Designer Tip**

*What Is Your Risk Profile?*

Before attempting to build risk profiles for others, it's always a good idea to start with yourself. Think of a risk invitation you recently encountered. What is your own risk-taking profile in terms of risk attitude, appetite, and tolerance? Does it change with different kinds of risks? When designing experiences for others, it can be extremely useful to have a thorough understanding of how you approach risk yourself. But it is also critical not to fall into risk

(*continued*)

affirmation bias and assume that your experiencers will automatically see it the same way. This can result in bad experience designs that backfire against all your best intentions. Knowing how you differ from your experiencers in terms of risk perception is a powerful hidden tool to develop, enabling you to see discomfort zone experiences more clearly from others' points of view.

## What Is the Fine Art of Failure?

In the art of "doing risk" and doing it well, we must reframe our attitudes about failure and consider it an essential part of the art of risk. As an experience designer, I not only anticipate the possibility of failure occurring with risk and plan to support people when it happens but have come to hope for it under certain circumstances. Why? We learn more from failure than from success, provided we fail forward. What does this mean and how can we do it?

> We must reframe our attitudes about failure and consider it an essential part of the art of risk.

Our attitudes toward failure occur in lockstep with our attitudes toward risk. If we are risk averse and hold a strong negative outcome bias, it often translates to a greater fear of failure. Through this lens, failure is considered something to be avoided at all costs. If failure happens, it is to be "fixed" immediately; and if that is not possible, it is to be denied, hidden, or minimized. To fail is a damning personal judgment and cause for embarrassment that reflects who we are. In this sense, failure is an identity threat, as in, "Are you a winner or are you a loser?" However, this is a false binary view of failure that splits the world and everyone in it into competitive terms of triumph or tragedy, good or bad, success or failure.

Earlier I mentioned that transformative experiences are invariably learning experiences in which we grow into a new understanding about ourselves and our place in the world. But how does this happen? Adopting a learning stance when we approach risk decisions within discomfort zones and then failing forward when risk outcomes skew negative are how this happens. The key idea here is that failure is not the opposite of success; it is part of success. Therefore, as designers, we need to become skilled in failing forward for ourselves and helping others to do so as well.

In his excellent book *Failing Forward*, leadership coach John Maxwell describes failures as essential stepping-stones that together build the road to success. This is not only related to how we think of risk and failure as individuals but powerfully applies to teams and organizations as well. For example, software developers using the popular Agile method will recognize this idea in their familiar prototyping mantra of "fail fast, fail often" in order to get to proven products more efficiently. The ability to "fail forward" allows us to free ourselves from the fear of completely negative consequences because we know we can learn something in the process, if we know how.

In our corporate leadership workshops, I often ask teams, "What is your risk culture?" That is, how their collective ideas about risk govern their thinking and actions around success, failure, talent, and innovation. These factors mutually create each other, and they are usually anchored on the leader's personal approach to risk.

For example, think of a team or group you have led or even currently lead. How would you describe your team's "risk culture" in whatever context it exists (business, tech, research, athletics, or even a family). Here are the five risk-failure stances I use in my workshops. Which one best describes how failure is thought of in your group when risk decisions come up?

1. Failure is not an option. It is avoided at all costs. If it occurs, it is considered a failure of the person in terms of their abilities, intelligence, or talent. Failure is shamed or hidden if it occurs.
2. If failure occurs, it is quietly minimized and not discussed for fear of embarrassment or destructive outcomes.
3. Failure is expected sometimes but not considered a reflection of a person's abilities, intelligence, or talent. People

are encouraged to "shake it off" and bounce back as
quickly as possible.

4. Failure is framed as a necessary learning experience.
   People are encouraged to think of it as normal and try to
   gain as much from it as they can, either on their own or
   through discussion with leaders or peers.

5. Failure is framed as a valuable learning experience, and
   there are multiple structured ways to adopt a growth
   mind-set, fully utilizing mistakes and negative risk
   outcomes designed into the team culture.

As ELVIS Experience Design Leaders, we can support strategic
personal and team-based risk taking by using failure to our advantage. In fact, some of the most innovative leaders I work with insist
that failures are maximized for their utility through well-structured
postmortem analyses. This strategy has been shown to effectively
boost employee engagement, retention, performance, resilience in the
face of mistakes, and perhaps most importantly, innovation and risk
taking. Additionally, in team cultures where failure has been transformed from catastrophe to growth opportunity and its stigma has
been defanged, it has fostered greater inclusion and diversity for both
marginalized and majority group members alike.

So what do these pro-growth failure attitudes and structures look
like? Here are the three simple yet powerful risk-failure pillars that
ELVIS Experience Design Leaders can and should do with their experiencers to promote failing forward:

1. Adopt a spirit of curiosity. Learning happens best when we
   bring a curious mind to the situation. As designers we can
   trigger this with the risk triplet calculus we explored
   above: "What can happen if I take this risk?" "How likely
   is that outcome?" and "What are the consequences if that
   outcome occurs?" But then add the crucial question:
   "What can I learn from this risk decision, given the
   different possible outcomes?" This is what I call the
   **Triplet+Learning** version of risk calculus.

2. Be strategic in risk decisions. When we ask, "What can I learn from this risk decision?" we open the doorway to strategic risk decisions. As designers, by guiding our experiencers through the Triplet+Learning questions when we present them with risk invitations, we can differentiate between risks that are reckless, irresponsible, or cavalier and those that are intentional and strategic and move us forward in some way, no matter the outcome.

3. Reframe mistakes into learning opportunities. People judge themselves harshly. If we judged our friends half as harshly as we judge ourselves, we wouldn't have any friends left. This is especially true when we make mistakes. However, when we frame them only as "failures," we can't see them as the learning opportunities they could be. I often get laughs when I quote the immortal painter Bob Ross: "We don't make mistakes. We have happy accidents." It's laughable because it is so naive sounding. But is it really? Not to view mistakes as learning experiences is the more naive way to live, in my view. The real failure is not to learn from failure.

### From Risk to Fail-Safe Identities

When we take this leadership stance toward mistakes and failures as a consistent part of transformative experience designs, we are helping our experiencers build *fail-safe* identities.

> "Fail-safe" does not mean completely "safe from failure" or "foolproof," as is commonly believed.

"Fail-safe" is an engineering term for a design feature that ensures success of the system even in the event of failures. It does not mean completely "safe from failure" or "foolproof" as is commonly believed. It is the capacity of the system to handle failures. In the context of ELVIS Experience Design Leadership, it is the art of presenting experiencers with risks that include the real possibility of failure, and then using that to help them forge new and more resilient identities. For corporate leaders to educators to parents and coaches, it is to forge experiencer identities as innovators and problem solvers, as people who know how to handle failure, learn from it, and use it to their advantage.

So how do we design for experiencers to build fail-safe identities? By putting identity-narrative creation at the center of your ELVIS designs and explicitly including elements that treat failure as growth opportunities. This brings us back to the Backwards Design method. When we consider what kind of narrative we hope our experiencers will ultimately translate their experiences into, we also need to consider what kind of identity narratives they will forge in relation to risk and failure. The values, skills, knowledge, strategy, and performance required to overcome failure all emanate and naturally flow from this central focus on identity narratives. Using Backwards Design, we see the process for this has common elements:

- Performance stems from attitude and ability
- Attitude and ability stem from experience
- Experience stems from developing a sense of agency to try new things
- Agency stems from identity narratives that include embracing risk, failure, and success
- And then we're back to performance as a learning process

> It is the role of the designer to present risks that stretch learners beyond their existing identities. The result is that success is redefined.

Incorporating fail-safe elements into the design of experiences means it is the role of the designer to present risk opportunities that will ultimately stretch learners beyond their existing identities, including opportunities for failure. After all, that is what risk is. And confronting failure is often a more valuable growth experience than succeeding, provided we have designed strategies for "failing forward" into the learners' experiences and identity development.

Think back on some of your mistakes and failures that you could not see as positive at the time but that wound up being absolutely critical. What value did they bring into your life? What new trajectories have your "failures" opened for you? What differences did they make in how you see yourself and how you treat failure in your life today?

The ultimate result of this perspective is that "success" for leaders, teachers, coaches, parents, and other experience designers is redefined. Success is no longer conflated with winning alone: "Our quarterly numbers outperformed the other teams." "My student got an A on the test." "We beat our rivals in the finals." "The United States takes the lead in medal count at the Olympics."

Rather, for ELVIS Experience Design Leaders, "success" is that their experiencers construct identities as endeavoring and independent learners who know how to struggle, take strategic risks, and internalize their own growth as a result, win or lose the event at hand. This kind of identity is one that will not only increase their performance over the long haul but also see them through the roller coaster of life and empower them to live more deeply because of it.

The knowledge that risk decisions and their outcomes are of value, whether positive or negative, and that we have tools to ensure learning occurs, liberates us to welcome our experiencers into their discomfort zones with greater confidence. It also sets us up to include considerations of who has control over risks (the next ELVIS element and the topic of the next chapter) in our ELVIS Experience Design Leadership.

## ELVIS Design Matrix Questions: Risk

1. **To what extent can experiencers make risk decisions within the experience? (For risk decisions to be valuable, they cannot be foisted on someone externally; they must come from within.)**
    1. Exposure to risk decisions is actively avoided or designed against.

2. Exposure to risk decisions is neither intended nor unintended. If it occurs, it is accidental.
3. There is at least one risk decision designed into the experience, with an emphasis on experiencer choice.
4. There are multiple opportunities for experiencers to make risk decisions, but the risks are not tailored to personal discomfort zones (areas where their sense of agency is low).
5. There are multiple opportunities for experiencers to make their own risk decisions, tailored to their personal discomfort zones.

2. **How would you describe the opportunities for experiencers to take physical risks? (Note that physical risks are associated with sensory experiences and do not necessarily present bodily harm potential.)**
   1. Exposure to physical risk is actively avoided or designed against.
   2. Exposure to physical risk is neither intended nor unintended. If it occurs, it is accidental.
   3. There is at least one option to take a physical risk designed into the experience.
   4. There are multiple opportunities for experiencers to take physical risks, but the risks are not tailored to personal discomfort zones (areas where their sense of agency is low).
   5. There are multiple opportunities for experiencers to take physical risks, tailored to their personal discomfort zones.

3. **How would you describe the opportunities for experiencers to take emotional risks? (Note that emotional risks are associated with feelings and attitudes, such as anger, disgust, fear, happiness, sadness, and surprise.)**
   1. Exposure to emotional risk is actively avoided or designed against.
   2. Exposure to emotional risk is neither intended nor unintended. If it occurs, it is accidental.

3. There is at least one option to take an emotional risk designed into the experience.

4. There are multiple opportunities for experiencers to take emotional risks, but not tailored to personal discomfort zones (areas where their sense of agency is low).

5. There are multiple opportunities for experiencers to take emotional risks, tailored to their personal discomfort zones.

4. **How would you describe the opportunities for experiencers to take intellectual risks? (Note that intellectual risks are associated with cognitive challenges involving memory, comprehension, reasoning, analyzing, and problem solving.)**

   1. Exposure to intellectual risk is actively avoided or designed against.

   2. Exposure to intellectual risk is neither intended nor unintended. If it occurs, it is accidental.

   3. There is at least one option to take an intellectual risk designed into the experience.

   4. There are multiple opportunities for experiencers to take intellectual risks, but not tailored to personal discomfort zones (areas where their sense of agency is low).

   5. There are multiple opportunities for experiencers to take intellectual risks, tailored to their personal discomfort zones.

5. **How would you describe the opportunities for experiencers to take social risks? (Note that social risks are associated with social harmony and conflict, such as a sense of belonging or exclusion, social acceptance or rejection, competition, hierarchy, dominance, inclusion, and solidarity.)**

   1. Exposure to social risk is actively avoided or designed against.

   2. Exposure to social risk is neither intended nor unintended. If it occurs, it is accidental.

3. There is at least one option to take a social risk designed into the experience.
4. There are multiple opportunities for experiencers to take social risks, but not tailored to personal discomfort zones (areas where their sense of agency is low).
5. There are multiple opportunities for experiencers to take social risks, tailored to their personal discomfort zones.

6. **To what extent are supports for failing forward integrated into the experience design?**
   1. Failure is not an option. It is avoided at all costs. If it occurs, it is considered a failure of the person in terms of their abilities, intelligence, or talent. Failure is shamed or hidden if it occurs.
   2. If failure occurs, it is quietly minimized and not discussed for fear of embarrassment or destructive outcomes.
   3. Failure is expected sometimes but not considered a reflection of a person's abilities, intelligence, or talent. Experiencers are encouraged to "shake it off" and bounce back as quickly as possible.
   4. Failure is framed as a necessary learning experience. Experiencers are encouraged to think of it as normal and try to gain as much from it as they can, either on their own or through discussion with leaders or peers.
   5. Failure is framed as a valuable learning experience, and there are multiple structured ways to adopt a growth mind-set, fully utilizing mistakes and negative risk outcomes designed into the experience.

Total for all questions: _____
ELVIS Zone (average score): _____

# 7 ■ Control

Who Has It, How to Strategically Give It Away, and Why

*Who looks outside, dreams; who looks inside, awakes.*

—Carl Jung

Control is the next Experiential Learning Variables & Indicators System element, the second of the ELVIS 7 (see figure 11). Control is all about choice—who has the choices and who makes the decisions. Control is part of the concept of agency, or our power to affect the course of events of an experience. Our sense of agency is how aware of that power we are, or what we believe ourselves to be capable of. Recall that our sense of agency is linked to how we define our discomfort zones and what we think is "risky" for us. Now, as we are about to discover, agency is also closely linked to our power of choice during an experience, which determines how much personal ownership we feel over an experience.

With the very title of "Experience Design Leader" or "Transformative Experience Designer" comes an assumption that control of

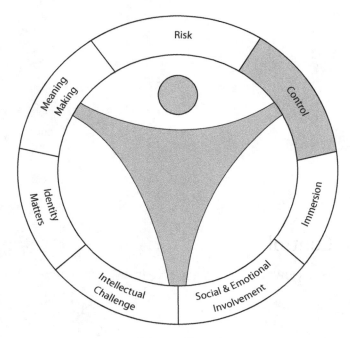

**Figure 11:** Control

the experience resides with the designer. And at first this is certainly true. However, we began this entire exploration of ELVIS Experience Design Leadership in the introduction by pointing out that transformative experiences come from within the experiencer and that as designers we are really in the business of designing *opportunities* for experiencers. That means creating the optimum conditions for transformative experiences to occur and presenting doorways that experiencers must walk through themselves. Those doorways are made of control.

Across nearly all transformative experiences, the experiencers in my work cite a transfer of control away from the designer and the design and toward the participants themselves as a critical element. In psychology this is related to the ideas of self-regulation and executive function, which we first explored in chapter 3. These are capacities of self-determination that begin to form in childhood when our parents hold the most control in our lives, and then expand as we grow toward becoming psychologically independent adults. Together, these processes allow us to shift control of our decisions and behaviors inward. When our ELVIS designs facilitate a similar process during a transformative experience, a new Self emerges from the experiencer and assumes new agency through the experience. To understand this better, let's look at how it happens as we grow up.

### *Carpe Sui*: Seize the Self

Internalizing the locus of control in our experiences is a big part of growing up. We all start out in the same place in life where the locus of control is external to us. Our parents or guardians have all the control, make all the decisions, and are responsible for us in every imaginable way. As we grow through childhood, we gradually take on the responsibility of making more decisions. However, the decisions we make are rooted in the desire to please our parents above all others. We channel what we think they want from us and try our best to make them proud, in most cases. Added to this are the expectations we feel from our teachers, coaches, and other caring adults in our lives.

It changes when we enter our teens, separate psychologically from our parents, and take on even more decisions. In these years, our friends and our peer-to-peer social interactions take priority in our lives. We also begin to experiment with our identities. As we do, we make most of our decisions based on these social pressures and what we think our friends will think. This again is known as "reflected self-appraisal" in identity theory, or what we think others think of us, which was introduced in chapter 4 as a powerful mechanism for self-esteem, confidence, and identity stability. The teen years are very sensitive and fragile for this reason. Here again we also see increasing prominence and increasing pressures from teachers, coaches, and other mentors in our lives, if not as much from our parents.

These early perspectives we hold about ourselves in relation to others, and whom to please with our decisions and our behaviors, are all external to us. That is, they are external sources of permission and validation. But in this mix, something new and wonderful happens (sometimes earlier, sometimes later); sources of permission shift inward and the locus of control in our lives gradually becomes internalized. It is the essence of coming of age to actually come to a deeper understanding of the Self and to live from that deeper wellspring source. At its perfect balance, this internalization of control results in an externally facing approach to leading our lives that is the familiar carpe diem spirit: "seize the day." But at heart, it is actually rooted by going inward to become *carpe sui*, "seize the Self," which is manifest when we finally and firmly grasp the controls of our unfolding trajectories.

> Internalization of control results in the familiar carpe diem spirit: "seize the day." But it is actually *carpe sui*, "seize the Self," when we finally grasp the controls of our unfolding trajectories.

Ironically, although assuming greater control in our lives is considered a normal part of growing up, it is also true that we often relinquish that same control and ownership of our lives to the well-worn routines, scripted roles, and societal structures in which we find ourselves as adults or, more precisely, in which we place ourselves. These take the form of the heavy burden of responsibilities to our loved ones, our jobs and incomes, our bosses, organizations, communities, and the professional and personal trajectories we have committed ourselves to. Feeling trapped as a passenger along for the ride rather than the pilot in control is a common feeling as the deep ruts of life's circumstances seem to fix us in place, an older cousin to the lack of self-determination we experience as children. When this happens, our professional adult lives become like a second childhood, where the sources of permission and control move once again to become external to us, or at least seem to.

A primary task in ELVIS Experience Design Leadership is to break experiencers (especially adults) out of this kind of scenario by incorporating a shift toward experiencer control into our designs. That is, we have to give control away by building experiencer agency—the power of choice and self-determination—into our designs. In practice, this means strategically and increasingly transferring power and choice in a designed experience to the experiencers themselves through each phase of the design: pre-experience, experience, and post-experience. How can we do this? Here are some simple ways:

- Pre-experience:
  - o Invite experiencers to help design methods for organizing cohorts. In my corporate team leadership workshops, we begin with mutually created agreements for team leadership (purpose and process).
  - o Design choice into how experiencers make preparations for the experience to come and invite them to share and compare. This could be approaches to learning new skills and strategies, collaboration, or even physical and mental preparation for tough challenges.
  - o Invite experiencers to help create and guide the narrative structures employed for a given experience. This can include creating group blogs, Slacks, Streams, podcasting, or old-fashioned journaling and group discussions. I use different combinations of these depending on cohort preferences.
- Experience:
  - o Explicitly discuss increasing control opportunities with your experiencers to gain their input and gauge their discomfort zones.
  - o Invite experiencers to help frame and design risks where appropriate.
  - o Include experiencers in building supports for failing forward as individuals and as a mutually supportive cohort.
- Post-experience:
  - o Structure experiencer-authored narrative construction, meaning making, and personal integration into the post-experience.

I often provide participatory design templates to team leaders I work with in order to guide these simple yet powerful leadership strategies. In many cases, leaders have already been applying similar tools without even realizing they were doing so. Together, we create customized approaches that fit their teams and their work. Visit the companion site for this book at DesigningTransformativeExperiences.com for some of these templates.

Expert game designer Will Wright knows all about the importance of experiencer choice and control. His seminal games SIM City, The Sims, Spore, and others are rooted in the psychology of problem solving and experiential learning. His pioneering work has influenced virtually all video game designers since, and these designers have become masters at providing experiencer agency in everything from avatar choice and appearance (costume, armor, hair, jewelry, style) to in-game decision-making, strategy, group play, and narrative contribution with multiple experience pathways and "endings" possible. In many ways, the entire challenge of designing transformative experiences can be thought of as designing multiple opportunities and multiple ways for experiencers to make choices and take control of the experience for themselves. Wright would call these "possibility spaces." As all seasoned leaders know, there are many pathways to success. As experience designers, we must embed experiencer options, alternatives, choices, and flexibility into our ELVIS designs. There must be lots of right answers whenever possible. Of course, this also means there will be lots of wrong answers, but that is a hallmark of good experiential learning.

Even for people who are used to taking charge and exerting control over situations in their lives, if we've done our job as designers in presenting risk invitations within their discomfort zones (situations where their sense of agency is low), then internalizing control in these new situations will still lead to growth and transformation. When we do this, experiencers not only participate more interactively in the experience but also contribute to its design for them.

There are two ways designers can facilitate this level of cocreation with experiencers: permission and participatory design. Let's take a look at each.

### Permission Is the Hidden Ancestor of Control: What I Learned Flying on Zero-G

Permission is the hidden ancestor of control. Permission always comes first. What kind of permission? Permission to participate, to think, to act, to engage, even to ponder, question, and explore. Without permission, control cannot be transferred from designers or claimed by experiencers. But where does permission come from, and how does it arrive? Just as with control, there are two kinds of permission we need to look at: external permission and internal permission. A large part of the job in ELVIS Experience Design Leadership is giving experiencers external permission to give themselves internal permission to participate, and thereby internalize control.

> ELVIS Experience Design Leadership involves giving experiencers external permission to give themselves internal permission to participate and thereby internalize control.

Let's look at the story of when I worked with NASA astronaut Story Musgrave and flew on the Zero-G aircraft with hundreds of educators. It is an example of an experience design that accommodated many different levels of permission on the part of participants.

From 2009 to 2010, I worked closely with the Northrop Grumman Foundation as a consultant on its Weightless Flights of Discovery program and directed a documentary film about it. In this innovative program, middle and high school educators from all over the United States were trained and flew on the Zero-G airplane, just like the training astronauts do for space flight. The Zero-G aircraft flies in giant parabolas, repeatedly climbing and diving over 10,000 feet, simulating, through free fall, the reduced gravity environment of space in the process. The whole program was a carefully designed experience, following the same phased outline I presented in chapter 5:

- Pre-experience: Teaming, training, learning safety and science, designing and planning experiments for flight, asking questions, beginning their narratives

- Experience: The actual flights, including flight-day pre-checks, optional motion-sickness medicines, conducting their experiments in flight, and landing and recovery
- Post-experience: Taking it all back to their students with new lessons, activities, narratives, and videos

With this design, the experience included several risk invitations to participants: to fly on a crazy roller-coaster Boeing 727 and the dangers that posed; to risk getting quite sick in flight (it's called the "vomit comet" for good reason); to collaborate with strangers on teams; to design flight experiments that could fail or may reveal one's lack of understanding of science; to invent new ways to bring it all back to their students; and to simply put themselves "out there" in front of their colleagues and students as they entered unknown discomfort zones and tried something entirely different from anything they had experienced before. All this was in service to create extraordinary experiences, generate rich narratives, build deeper identities as teachers, and then transfer that excitement and boldness and sense of adventure to their students. Who knows what could happen when we do that?

Consulting on the project with me was famed astronaut Story Musgrave. If you don't know of Story, the best way I can describe him is as a modern-day renaissance man with the fire of a child and the wisdom of a sage. Among other things, he is an artist, a poet, an engineer, a pilot, a flight instructor, a skydiving instructor, an author, a neurosurgeon, and a six-time space shuttle astronaut. He was the architect and lead space walker of the missions that captured and repaired the Hubble Space Telescope when it was discovered that its mirrors were deformed. He is a very insightful guy.

Story helped me understand the similarities and differences between what I experienced flying on Zero-G with the educators and the realities of space travel, including living and working with others in space. He spoke of developing an intuitive sense for being in microgravity. "You have to give yourself over to the experience," he said. "Become one with it. I love being in space. I never got space motion sickness and I never got tired of it," he told me. "I feel I belong there. I'm at home in it."

As we worked with the teachers, Story and I observed that most held similar attitudes of giving themselves "over to the experience." They gave themselves internal permission to engage. In many ways they made the experience their own. I had teams of teachers who designed their own mission patches for their flights, just as astronauts do for space missions. I had teachers who included their students in the design of their flight experiments and kept blogs for their students. I had teachers who created mini-documentaries of their experiences and chronicled how they brought it back to their classrooms. I even used clips of their videos in the "official" documentary I was directing. In short, through their internal permission to participate fully, they internalized the locus of control of the experience and forged personal ownership of it, approaching the risks with a positive childlike sense of wonder.

"I think teachers as a class are more open and excited about a new experience," Story remarked. "They almost need to be able to have that innocent reaction to an experience in order to be good teachers."

There were also teachers who did not fully engage in the experience. Some avoided the teamwork. Some decided to stay seated on the flight and not float freely or tumble through space. Others skipped doing the experiments or learning the science, choosing to do just the flight itself. Some did not try to incorporate the experience into their teaching with their students.

I worked closely both with teachers who fully engaged and with those who did not, interviewing them extensively before, during, and after their experience; surveying them; visiting their classrooms postexperience to examine how the experience changed their teaching; working with their students to learn how impressions of their teachers had changed; examining whether and how their choices regarding other areas of risk had changed; and asking them how their own self-perceptions evolved after enough bake time had elapsed for durable meaning making. The result was that we can learn something very important about permission and control by looking at why some participants engage with or disengage from our experience designs.

Those who engage very often have a mind-set that allows them to grant internal permission to participate. This may be because the experience is not too far into their discomfort zones or because they are quite cognizant of the opportunity it presents precisely *because* it is well *within* their discomfort zones and they have decided to go there. This is "answering the call to adventure," a mind-set that we of course try to incubate in our ELVIS designs as we frame and prime our participants for the risks. For Zero-G, the experience was presented as follows: "This is as close to being an astronaut as you may get." For many STEM educators, that is almost like an irresistible drug. As one of my participants put it a few days before his flight, "If the plane were outside right now, we'd all run to get on it. It's like, I can't believe someone is giving me the chance to do this!"

However, those who disengage with an experience are processing permission differently. There are typically two subtle but important things going on when experiencers choose not to engage fully with an experience design.

First, looking at the Zero-G flights as an example, as you might expect, some experiencers did not give themselves internal permission to engage in all aspects of the experience despite the external permission and the many invitations and expectations incorporated into the design. With any given cohort of people, this happens. Not everyone will jump on board right away, and some may not jump on board at all. And that is OK. It is often related to self-esteem or concerns for safety. Not all the experiences you design or all the parts included within them will resonate with everyone. It will sometimes be too deep into their discomfort zones, inviting them to risks they are unable or unwilling to give themselves permission to take. In some cases, experiencers may not even recognize that there is an opportunity to give internal permission.

Second, experiencers can also give themselves permission to *not* fully engage. This is about decisively saying, "I choose not to." With the Zero-G flights, for example, some people decided not to unlatch the seatbelt and float about wildly in the disorienting tumble of free fall. They did the risk calculus, assessed other factors involved, and opted out. There is a fuzzy boundary between not giving oneself permission to engage and giving oneself explicit permission to *not* engage.

> When transformative experiences occur, control over the experiences moves toward the experiencer.

The important thing for designers to know is that when transformative experiences occur, control over the experiences moves toward the experiencer. While this usually happens when someone gives themselves affirmative permission to fully engage with what we have designed, it can also happen when someone internalizes control to *not* fully engage. Or to put it another way, follow the control; when control over the experience shifts toward the experiencer, it is far more likely that a transformative experience will occur, whether the experiencer gives themselves permission to fully engage or permission not to. In any case, when control remains mostly in the hands of the designer, it is far less likely that a transformative experience will occur. I like to think of it as a permission continuum (see figure 12).

As ELVIS designers, we need to do two things:

1. Create experience designs that accommodate different permission situations, allowing for a variety of responses to your risk invitations. In the case of Zero-G, the experience design accommodated each of these internal permission situations, and participants got out of it according to how they let themselves get into it.
2. Shift control to our experiencers, either gradually or quickly depending on the situation. Again, we do this best

Permission

Designer Controls                                    Experiencer Controls

**Figure 12:** Permission Continuum

with direct dialogue, making them consciously aware of where their permissions and controls are and where they need to go. I routinely do this with my ELVIS designs, including embedded reflections, interviews, group sessions, and think-alouds that make their thinking visible to themselves and others.

As designers, we must frequently ask ourselves, "How can I best move experiencers toward the 'full permission to participate' end of the continuum?" For example, there is a hidden boundary between experience designers who grant external permission to experiencers and offer positive invitations and encouragement (all in the sweet spot of ELVIS designs), and experience designers who cross over into

---

### Designer Tip

#### *Make an Invitation of Control*

When presenting risk invitations to experiencers, avoid one-size-fits-all approaches. Instead, the goal is to invite experiencers to help control the experience, to choose and shape it interactively. Include the following key questions (asked from the experiencer's point of view) in discussions with your experiencers. And keep in mind that you are seeking an incremental shift of control for each of the different flavors of risk that experiencers may encounter in your design.

- Where does control of the risk experience seem to reside right now? How and when can I move that control inward?
- What kind of permission (external and internal) is needed for me to engage?
- What do I need in order to grant myself internal permission to participate?
- How can I contribute to the design of the risk for myself, if I can?
- What are my options for controlling things during the experience if I need to? Can I ask for help? Can I join others? Can I go alone? Can I change my mind?

exerting negative pressure, which can lead to coercion, manipulation, and feelings of embarrassment or shame (definitely *not* where we want to go). Again, our job is to create and open doorways. It is up to the people to cross the threshold.

Overall, the original vision for the Weightless Flights of Discovery program was to excite teachers with immersive STEM learning and to inspire them to take on an adventurous identity beyond that of the typical educator. The experience designers I worked with at Northrop Grumman (Sandra Evers-Manly and Cheryl Horn) and at Zero-G (Michelle Peters and Matt Reyes, among many others) did a wonderful job. It was an amazing success for most of the experiencers. As I often do as part of my research into transformative experiences, I followed many of these teachers for years after their flights were completed to see how the experience continued to affect them and how durable the impacts may be. The program changed the lives of hundreds of educators nationwide, impacting how they taught, how their students perceived them, and how they perceived themselves—transformation in action.

As powerful as this example was, when permission is coupled with an invitation for experiencers to contribute to the experience design itself, we gain another tool for transformative experiences.

### Participatory Design: An Invitation to Sit at the Design Table

Sometimes control transfer happens in the pre-experience design phase, and many times it happens in real time (in situ) while an experience is occurring. In both cases, this is known as "participatory design" in educational psychology and leadership theory, and it is used in many creative processes today.

For us, it embodies the idea that designing an experience is not something we do *to* our participants or even *for* them but is rather something we do *with* them. Therefore, the designer's role is shifted from one of authority or expert to one of facilitator or host. By inviting experiencers to the design table, we open the floodgates for their creative energies to be released and for greater possibilities of making the experience personally relevant to them.

Employing participatory design strategies into our leadership approach is the beginning of transferring control of an experience to the experiencers themselves. In fact, when you use strategies for the codesign of experiences, experiencer participation then becomes part of the larger experience itself. Here is a 4-Step Participatory Design process I've used in the pre-experience design phase:

1. Context-Setting Discussion: The scope and scale of the experience opportunity, including the possibilities, goals, and potential outcomes, are laid out so that everyone is on the same page right from the beginning.
2. Divergent Creative Process: This is commonly known as brainstorming, where ideas are quickly generated with no critiques and no eliminations at this stage. Here we want a "yes, and . . ." approach from everyone rather than a "no, but . . ." approach. This can be applied to any design phase or component of your experience.
3. Convergent Creative Process: Here critiques and eliminations are welcome and encouraged. Ideas from the previous step are whittled down to the most usable ones. In this step, emergent or slightly tweaked ideas often come to the fore.
4. Select and Refine: The designer guides the group to the final selection of ideas that hold the most promise. Note that this step may occur after a reflection period for everyone to gain some perspective before final contributions. It can also include important questions and concerns that may or may not be answerable at that time.

When participatory design happens in real time during the experience phase (rather than the pre-experience phase), it is usually less structured owing to the simple lack of time. However, if you've built narrative creation and embedded reflection strategies into your experience design (chapter 12), then these provide excellent opportunities for adapting a design in situ.

For example, I will often use planned group discussions and meaning-making forums to pose design questions: "Tomorrow we will face a big challenge. Let's discuss the risks you see and how we

**Designer Tip**

*Participatory Design Tips*
- Allow multiple voices to be heard and involved in the design, resulting in experiences and outcomes that suit a wider range of users.
- Hear each other's ideas, fears, concerns, and hopes. The process builds empathy and positive cohort effects (more in chapter 9).
- Create greater buy-in, personal ownership, and investment in the experience.
- Generate greater personal relevance for each experiencer involved by bringing their different identities directly into the design process, rather than trying to learn about their identities externally and then design accordingly for them.

might modify our plans to make the most of the potential outcomes." And then be ready to make changes to what you have planned to the extent possible. These are also opportunities to bring in newly acquired data or lessons learned from some earlier part of the experience. These may be the results of some team effort (how did we do in our last competition?), a product or prototype (what user data did we get from the last rapid deployment?), or the health and safety of your group (do we need a helicopter evacuation for Sam?). In all cases, design flexibility is a key concept in participatory design. It will not work and may even backfire if your attitude and design are authoritarian and rigid.

### Controlling Your Shift of Control
Here I must dispel a powerful myth. A rookie mistake that many new designers make is to transfer too much control over the experience to experiencers and to do it too soon. The trick is balance, doing it at the right time and in the right way, which requires knowing your audience's capabilities combined with your own design skill and design tools so it does not backfire. To see how, let's look at two simple examples.

First, imagine that you have a group of 10-year-olds who want to build a zip-line obstacle course in the backyard (yes, a true story). If you begin by simply transferring all the control for this experience to the kids right from the start, the project will likely end with a trip to the emergency room. If the reason is not clear to you, then you either are not a parent or were never a 10-year-old. However, a gradual transfer of control from you to them as they gain perspective on the balance between fun, challenge, and safety provides a growth pathway design through which the kids earn independence with your guidance. Learning takes place, an understanding of controlled danger emerges, and hospital visits are hopefully eliminated.

Now imagine you are training a group of junior executives, mostly young white men in their 30s, to become mentors and sponsors to employees who are members of marginalized groups as part of the company's diversity, equity, and inclusion program (also a true story). If you begin by laying out the program's goals and timelines and then immediately transfer all the control of the experience to the junior execs, who have no actual experience doing this kind of thing, the effort will likely end with disillusioned execs, pissed-off mentees, and maybe even a few lawsuits. However, if you gradually transfer control of the experience to the junior execs, as well as to those whom they mentor, through proper preparation on the differences between mentors and sponsors and how to use research-based approaches for mentoring people who are marginalized in one or more ways, you again provide a growth pathway design.

These are two relatively commonplace scenarios; both experiences are true, but neither was designed to be transformative. It seems painfully obvious in these situations that transferring total control to the participants right away is a bad decision with bad outcomes. The same is true in transformative experiences, however, even though it may not seem as obvious that a gradual shift of command and control is needed. Why? Because too often people assume that since transformative experiences are so personal and so subjective, control over them must begin and end with the experiencer. After all, we keep saying transformative experiences come from within us, right? But this design philosophy of total control transfer can lead to a very passive and hands-off approach of the designer if we are not careful. Don't mistake an abdication of your role as designer for effective transfer of control over an experience to the experiencers.

> Don't mistake an abdication of your role as designer for effective transfer of control to the experiencers.

As ELVIS designers, we must consider our audience's needs and abilities when deciding how and when to best transfer control to them, and then implement a gradual and strategic transfer of control to ensure that a learning experience takes place versus pushing people off a cliff before they are ready to fly. This can only be done through frequent dialogue and an explicit invitation to help guide their own experience.

As we gradually do this more, the invitation becomes unnecessary; experiencers will internalize greater control without waiting for an invitation. When this happens, it is a very good sign, provided we as designers are hoping and expecting to "lose" control in this way. As designers, our job is often to work ourselves out of a job in this sense. Indeed, in some cases, the internalization of permission and control extends well beyond the designed experience.

### Emergence in Control: When Permission Ripples beyond the Design

The most durable impacts from some of my designed experiences did not just emerge from the specific risks and controls I included. Lasting effects often emanate from changes in *how* experiencers think about and act on risk decisions and control. When the internal permission and control that they have realized within your ELVIS designs later extends beyond the context of the designed experience and into experiencers' lives broadly, we see the emergence of undesigned experiential elements, or ripple effects. Sometimes the ripple effects themselves become the transformative experience.

Consider three different examples of tremendous ripple effects from three people who had the same designed experience on my Tanzanian expeditions. For each person, newly discovered permission and control during their journeys ultimately led to different kinds of agency in their lives beyond the experience.

Carrie was a young woman from a small town in the Midwest. She had married young and settled into a quiet life with no children, not much travel, and not much exposure to the wide world beyond her front door. But she harbored a silent wanderlust. When the opportunity to travel to Africa came, it was almost as if she had been waiting for it.

Daniel was a middle-aged man with a great deal of wilderness adventure experience already behind him when he journeyed to Africa with me. He had traveled. He had married young as well and also had a daughter. The prospect of climbing Mount Kilimanjaro was what drew Daniel to this new experience.

Jay was a middle-aged, elementary school music teacher also from the Midwest. He journeyed to Africa with a healthy spirit of adventure and a thirst for discovering the music and cultures of Tanzania.

For Carrie, the adventure ushered in a series of profound life changes. She had her eyes opened on the journey. Everything was new, from traveling internationally to exploring the Serengeti to using restrooms with no seats. For a month, being away from everything that was familiar unlocked Carrie's internal permission to inhabit what she called her "truest identity." This was a Self who saw the world through large eyes with deeper perspectives than those considered normal where she lived. "In a place where life revolved around football and snowmobiling, transnational values were not understood or welcome," she told me. In Africa, she permitted herself to prioritize what had previously been stifled in her heart: simplicity, compassion, and caring more for people than for things. And, for the first time she was with a social cohort who validated this worldview instead of thinking it strange. Early on, she knew it would not be a onetime trip for her. She could feel the tide rising in her life.

For Daniel, being on an adventure was familiar territory, although Kilimanjaro was the catalyst he came for. He was looking for a challenge that would push him, and Kili did not disappoint. Although the climb is not considered technical and requires no special equipment, the volcano is very high and is a seven-day trek. Altitude sickness, exhaustion, and freezing-cold temperatures are all on the menu. Daniel suffered his way to the icy, windy summit, declaring on the top, "This was so much harder than I expected. But if I can do this, I can do anything." Little did we know what that would mean for him back home.

Jay was on a mission of pure exploration through singing, dancing, drumming, hand clapping, instruments, lyrics, stories, and more. And yet, he felt a little isolated during the journey as the only music educator. One day as we hiked high above the clouds on Kili, he said to me, "Brad, what am I supposed to do with this whole experience back home? I have no idea." And yet, two months after the journey was over, he used the experience to do something amazing for his community.

Two months after the journey, as is customary when I lead those kinds of experiences, the entire cohort reconvened to participate in a film festival to showcase their personal documentaries of the journey. At this two-day event inside an old gothic theater, each person would introduce their film by contextualizing how the experience had affected their life upon returning.

When Carrie introduced her film, we learned of the deep impact the experience had on her and the disconnect she was feeling in her life back home as a result. We learned that she was already planning a return trip to Africa, but this time she intended to live like a local, not a traveler passing through. She made arrangements to live with our guide and his family and to work with St. Timothy's school in Moshi, a place we had visited. She returned to Africa within the year. During her second stay, she crossed a tremendous threshold. "Africa broke open the box of my life. Every bit of me poured out. I took off the blinders and could finally see where I wanted to be and what my path should be. I wanted to speak MY voice into the world." Unable to go back to her old life, Carrie ended her marriage. She later fell in love with the younger brother of our African guide. They married and today split their time between Tanzania and the United States, raising beautiful twin boys and carving out a life of freedom to be themselves together.

When Daniel got up to introduce his film, people expected his usual playful, up-for-anything spark. Instead, he began weeping. "There's no way you could've known, but for the past year my life has been falling apart." He went on to explain how his wife of many years had become addicted to opioids, meth, and alcohol and how he was desperately trying to find the right way through it—for him, for her, and for their young daughter. Like Carrie, Daniel found that being away in Africa gave him the shift in perspective and permission he needed to act. But climbing Kili revealed the inner strength he was looking for. Daniel used the journey and the ordeal of climbing the mountain as propulsion to cross his own threshold. Coming home, he finally gave himself permission to orchestrate an intervention for his wife, assembling her entire family and set of close friends (past and present) to confront her with love as well as demand that she make a series of agreements to heal herself. "Kili," he said, "saved my family."

When Jay came home, he solved the problem of how to translate the experience for his students and his community. He wrote an original musical production wherein each of his fifth- and sixth-grade choir kids played the part of one of the people on the Africa adventure, reenacting all the drama, hardship, excitement, failures, and triumphs right there on stage. He even excerpted entries from the journals of his fellow travelers (with their support, of course) to create the script. Three hundred people from his community came to the performance. Afterward, I interviewed some of his students:

*I never thought that anyone I knew, someone from my school, would ever be able to go to Africa and climb Mount Kilimanjaro. And definitely not a teacher.*

*I think it's so great because he went to Africa, then we got to go to Africa on stage, and then everyone who came to the show, they got to go to Africa through seeing it and maybe they will be inspired by it too and tell other people.*

*I think maybe I could go climb a mountain now. Maybe Kiliman-jaro. Maybe Mount Everest.*

Jay used his experience to inspire entire families and his colleagues. In fact, he remarked that the work of putting the musical production together in that way actually enriched his overall experience (a facet of meaning making we will cover in chapter 12).

These three examples demonstrate three kinds of agency emerging from, and going beyond, the designed experience:

1. Agency development: Carrie's emergent experience was one of sheer *carpe sui* agency development, as she took full control over her life and its direction as a result of the internal permission and control she tapped into in Africa. Hers is a coming-of-age and empowerment narrative with identity impacts that crossed a threshold. She could not go back to her old life; she could only go forward. As she described her validation of a long-buried self-view, "Life doesn't have to be about what you don't have and what's wrong. I am grateful for the abundance in my life. True abundance is not things. It is your heart being content and being able to be real and to treasure the people around you with passion for life and zest for love."

2. Agency extension: Daniel's emergent experience was one of propulsion to do something he eventually discovered he could not *not* do. After years of anxious uncertainty, through a struggle to the very top of an ancient volcano, he found a rebirth of belief into what he was capable of—and the promise of Self to try. His is a narrative of test of will. Whether he succeeded or not with his wife's intervention, Daniel extended his agency on the proving slopes of Kilimanjaro.

3. Agency-lending: Through his production, Jay expertly generated agency-lending for his students and the

community. His is a narrative of inspiration and agency-lending. Agency-lending (or agency transfer) is what occurs when a mentor transfers a sense of capacity to a protégé. For example, the protégé sees the mentor doing something (or even just hears about something the mentor has done) that is currently beyond the protégé's ability, and then thinks, "Hey . . . you did that and I know you, you're not that different from me, so maybe I can do that too." The power of the affiliation the protégé feels for the mentor makes it work. This is the essence of effective role modeling. Protégés recognize the similarities between themselves and their mentors, and through storytelling come to see pathways to a similar destination. They grow a sense of aptitude, potential, or self-efficacy for taking that same journey. In Jay's case, this became a literal truth as, years later, some of those same students decided to retrace his steps in Africa for themselves.

In each of these cases, the designed experience was the trigger that invited each of them into larger and more authentic conversations with themselves. We see different emergent experiences resulting from the same designed itinerary because the identities and life circumstances of the experiencers going in were very different. The experience design opened the doorway, and these people gave themselves permission to walk through. In each case, Africa was a catalyst for internalizing control as different forms of agency, control they brought home with them and that caused emergent ripple effects in their lives that went beyond anything I could've possibly designed for or imagined. In the end, it was the ripple effects that became the bigger transformative experience.

> It caused emergent ripple effects in their lives that went beyond anything I could've designed for or imagined.

What is the take-home message for designers? It is simply this: the *ways* you present risk invitations and the ways you support your experiencers in assuming greater control and permission in the experience are more important than the risks themselves. The risk opportunities will come and go with the designed events you have arranged. But the personal processes for *how* experiencers face those challenges can extend beyond your design. Accommodating this in your ELVIS designs requires a departure from traditional leadership models.

---

### Designer Tip

#### *Design for Co-control Ripple Effects*

- Instead of keeping total control and trying to design around every corner and for every possible failure associated with risks, ask, "What are the opportunities here (for any given risk) to transfer permission and control to my experiencers?" Invite experiencers to consider this question with you. Together, look for ways they can personalize their experience.

- Instead of prescribing the "permissible" ways and methods experiencers can and should take control of the experience for themselves, ask, "How can we explore the process of assuming more control and make it a very explicit part of the design?" Unpacking external permission and internal permission as precursors to internalizing control is an important component to discuss with your experiencers. It gives them insights into what gifts the experience could reveal to them and invites their own creativity via participatory design.

- Consider the design elements that facilitate the transfer of permission and control beyond the experience. These are elements of structured reflection, meaning making, narration, and sharing within the design that make this kind of emergence possible. Examples include group and individual discussions, journaling, blogging, and more. For the case of the Africa experience, the personal documentary films and sharing them at the film festival served this purpose. I explicitly asked them to include how their journey to Africa changed their lives back home, if it did.

- Seek a dynamic balance of control between the design and the experiencer that allows for changing levels of permission and freedom in risk decisions, the social and emotional experience, and meaning-making methods both as it happens and afterward in retrospect.

---

**ELVIS Design Questions: Control**
1. **Who has most of the control over the experience in general? (A transfer of control toward the experiencer, whether quickly or gradually, is a hallmark of transformative experiences.)**
    1. The experience designer (leader, educator, parent, or coach) has the most control over the experience.
    2. The experience designer (leader, educator, parent, or coach) controls the big-picture goals and objectives, but experiencers have some control over their own actions.
    3. The experience designer (leader, educator, parent, or coach) and the experiencers share control of the experience equally and in collaboration.
    4. Experiencers have input and some control over both the big-picture goals and objectives as well as the specific actions they engage in.
    5. Experiencers have the most control over the experience, including setting the big-picture goals and objectives as well as the specific actions they engage in. The experience designer (leader, educator, parent, or coach) functions as a facilitator, helper, or embedded guide.
2. **What are the sources of permission for experiencers to make decisions and take action within the experience?**
    1. The source of permission is external to the experiencers. The experience designer (leader, educator, parent, or coach) is usually the source of permission.
    2. The source of permission is mostly external to the experiencers, residing mostly, but not entirely, with the experience designer.
    3. The source of permission is equally internal and external to the experiencers, with permission shared between experiencers and the designer.
    4. The source of permission is mostly, but not entirely, internal to the experiencers. The experience designer (leader, educator, parent, or coach) has some permission power.

5. The source of permission to make decisions and take action is internal to the experiencers.

3. **What are the sources of permission for experiencers to engage with others during the experience, including when and how?**

   1. The source of permission for social engagement is external to the experiencers. The experience designer (leader, educator, parent, or coach) is usually the source of permission.

   2. The source of permission is mostly external to the experiencers, residing with the experience designer, but not entirely. For example, leaders may decide when but not how, or vice versa.

   3. The source of permission for social engagement is equally internal and external to the experiencers, with permission shared between experiencers and the designer.

   4. The source of permission is mostly, but not entirely, internal to the experiencers. The experience designer (leader, educator, parent, or coach) has some permission power.

   5. The source of permission for social engagement is internal to the experiencers. Experiencers decide when and how to engage with others during the experience.

4. **How would you describe experiencers' "personal ownership" of the experience in terms of their ability to contribute to its design and/or implementation?**

   1. Experiencers have no personal ownership of the experience, with no control over the design or implementation.

   2. Experiencers have some limited personal ownership of the experience. For example, they may have control over its implementation but not its design.

   3. Personal ownership of the experience is shared equally between experiencers and the designer for both design and implementation.

4. Experiencers have high personal ownership of the experience and are able or even invited to contribute to its design and/or implementation.

5. Experiencers have the most personal ownership and investment in the experience, in terms of both its design and implementation. In many cases, the experiencers *are* the experience designers.

Total for all questions: _____

ELVIS Zone (average score): _____

# 8 ■ Immersion

Multisensory and Imaginative Design Strategies

*The old pond*
*A frog leaps in.*
*Sound of the water.*

—Basho

The third ELVIS Design Matrix element also crosses all transformative experiences. It is the degree and type of immersion an experience includes (see figure 13). Generally speaking, the greater the immersion, the more powerful the experience. There are two broad categories for this experiential variable that I use in my ELVIS designs, and both contribute to immersive experiences: multisensory immersion and imaginative immersion. Since the senses are more straightforward, let's begin with them.

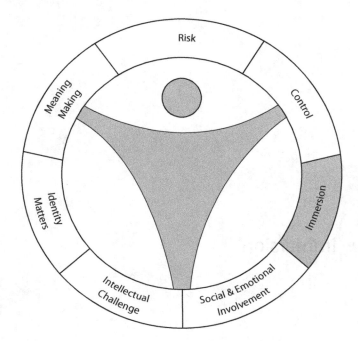

**Figure 13:** Immersion

## What Is Multisensory Immersion?

We are most familiar with the standard five senses we learn about in school: seeing, hearing, smelling, tasting, and touching. And these are a good place for us to start thinking about immersive experiences. But we also need to acknowledge that we actually have many more senses, some of which are combinations.

Most important is our kinesthetic sense, telling us about the movement, action, and orientation of our bodies in space. This includes balance and acceleration sensed by the micro-organs of the vestibular system in the inner ear, combined with proprioception, or the sense of how our body parts are oriented in space and in relation to each other, detected through gravity sensors located in our joints and other places. You can think of the kinesthetic sense like our own internal gyroscope and accelerometer all in one.

We also have other senses: pain, pleasure, stress, temperature, thirst, hunger, fullness, and even time passing. The wonderful thing about our senses, of course, is how they combine to provide us with much more than the sum of their parts.

How do our senses contribute to immersion? Think of a movie you love. How many physical senses are engaged when you watch it? Two: seeing and hearing. Add in a nice theatrical sound system. Sometimes the lower-frequency sound and music may rumble your seat, and you can feel that. Now throw in some popcorn and a soda at the theater (or at home), and you can taste those. Suddenly you have a multisensory moviegoing experience—a big reason we like to go to theaters and make our home viewing more like a theater experience.

Now how about a ride at Disneyland or another theme park? They involve all the same senses as watching a movie plus the kinesthetic sense, often with surprising motions and feelings. Consider some of their more creative ones, like *Star Wars Rise of the Resistance*, in which you move through the bad guys' lair and interact with characters, space ships come and go, characters battle using light sabers and laser blasters, and more. Or the ride *Pandora the World of Avatar*, which includes sitting astride a flying Banshee with wind in your hair, ocean spray in your face, stunning visuals, and strange motions that can only be described as an airborne living rocket motorcycle.

Next think of a video game you love (if you play video games). Whether it's an old 1980s game like Pac-Man or a modern multi-person role-playing game like Roblox or Fortnite, it likely includes three physical senses when you play it: seeing, hearing, and touching the controller. Now add in a controller that rumbles in your hands according to the game's events. Next, add in a gaming chair that rumbles and has built-in speakers and maybe even lights up. Finally, throw in a virtual reality headset designed to surround the senses and create visio-vestibular illusions that are almost as good as flight simulators that actually toss and turn.

Finally, consider a simple walk in the woods, which for me beats them all for a deep and rich immersive experience. From the soft crunch of the trail underfoot to the warm sunshine dappling through pine needles overhead. From the sweet smell of fresh air in your nose and filling your lungs, to the birdsong, the beating of your own heart, and the smile on your face. While the other examples all take advantage of our naturally evolved capacities for multisensory experiences, a walk in the woods is what we evolved those senses for.

And now (and I'm sorry to do this to you), think of sitting in an office hunched over your computer and your phone. If it's any consolation, that's what I am doing right now in writing this, although I've added a favorite breakfast tavern and a warm chai to the mix to keep my other senses alive. It is no wonder that the poorly designed experiential modes most of us deal with for work or school simply cannot compete with the level of engagement that multisensory immersion brings. It's why kids like recess more than class. It's why working adults need vacations that involve expansions in sensory experience, such as adventure travel, "beaching it," ski trips, and the like. If we can't change the plight of our sensory-deprived work and school environments, we are forced to seek a semblance of balance through such countermeasures.

Real-time neural imaging, such as functional MRI (magnetic resonance imaging), has been increasingly used to research learning over the past 15 years. It involves the collaboration of experts in education, psychology, and cognitive neuroscience to look directly at live brain scans of people while they are learning, revealing a number of benefits.

The combination of a greater number of multisensory inputs and the greater depth and variety within our senses can generate rich and captivating experiences. Multisensory design causes the activation of multiple brain centers in sequence and in synchronicity as experiencers gather and process these inputs, both consciously and unconsciously.

Such neural activation and networking are strongly linked to holistic experiential learning modes that include increased focus, heightened sense of awareness, motivation, powerful emotions, stronger memory formation, and impacts on our investment and ownership in an experience—all important elements for transformative experiences. Our capacity to have transformative experiences in our lives is partially determined by our engagement through multiple senses and on multiple levels.

> Our capacity to have transformative experiences is partially determined by our engagement through multiple senses and on multiple levels.

For experience designers, I always recommend that designers examine their experiences from the experiencer's point of view. Therefore, two questions emerge:

1. How can I increase the number of senses engaged?
2. How can I deepen the experience of the senses that are engaged?

Many people assume that doing these two things requires exotic travel, getting really dirty, or confronting immense challenges. Many designs take experiencers into the wild for dramatic personal close encounters with their discomfort zones, such as many of my own. But so powerful is the effect of multisensory experience that we need not go to those kinds of extraordinary efforts as Experience Design Leaders to deeply and positively impact our experiencers. Let me give you a very powerful example.

### What I Learned about Personal Immersion through Intersectionality

I once attended a conference hosted by the National Science Foundation on building more inclusive cultures in professional environments. Before my own session, I was lucky enough to participate in an activity led by a team from the Science Museum of Minnesota, who had been working on a project dubbed the Geography of Identity and the psychological concept of intersectionality. This is a term originally coined by law professor Kimberlé Crenshaw to describe the challenging experiences of people who occupy multiple marginalized identity categories simultaneously (like being a woman and being Black in corporate America), where the barriers to meaningful careers are amplified in difficulty and frequency. Intersectionality is related to the ideas we discussed in chapter 4 around multiple identity types. The idea has since grown to become important in diversity, equity, and inclusion work.

The talented presenters from Minnesota on this day had us each draw a vertical line on a piece of paper representing race. The topmost end of the line represented what was dominant or normative in society and was where power and privilege were found. The bottom-most part of the line represented what was "other" according to the dominant perspective and held the least power and privilege. Then we drew more lines for ethnicity, dis/ability, class, age, gender, sexual orientation, spirituality, and more—all elements that contribute to our sense of self and all intersecting in the center, where we live. Finally, we drew a horizontal line through it all, representing power and privilege across the board, where the farther above the line you fell on each dimension the more advantaged you were in society, and the farther below the line you fell on each dimension the more disadvantaged you were.

As our identity diagrams took shape, we had multiple colored identity lines all intersecting in the middle with small dots locating us according to the advantage line—a wonderful snapshot of our own personal intersectional selves.

But the exercise was not over. We were then asked to draw such a diagram for ourselves from ten years earlier and one for the present and then compare them, because people change as they age and gain experience.

Next, we partnered up, facing our chairs to each other closely and sitting directly opposite our partners, kneecaps to kneecaps. We were first invited to simply gaze at each other in silence for two minutes. If you have never done something like this before, gazing at a complete stranger for two minutes is a wonderfully awkward and humbling experience. And two minutes is a long time.

We then introduced ourselves (first names only) and took turns explaining our intersectionality diagrams to each other. Each person had five minutes uninterrupted to do so. Finally, we had time for questions and discussion before we had to present our partner's ideas of their intersectionality to the larger group.

It was a powerful experience for many reasons. From a designer's point of view, the experience simply combined presentation mode with a drawing activity and then partner discussions. That is, three senses were engaged: seeing and hearing through the leader's presentation and our work with partners, plus touching and tactile engagement through the activity of creating our brightly colored diagrams. But the depth and richness within those activated senses and what that meant was what made the difference. The exercise was immersive because of the very personal ways our senses were engaged. All these years later, I still remember the intimate feelings of connection, empathy, and vulnerability from simply gazing at my partner before we began our dialogue and the new perspectives the entire exercise gave me as I moved from theoretically understanding intersectionality (as an identity researcher) to a lived experience that I owned. All made possible through immersion.

### Spotlight-Floodlight Immersive Design Strategies

Multisensory immersive design is about much more than simply piling on the number of senses we can engage within our experiencers. In fact, that can backfire and cause sensory overload, distraction, difficulty of focus, stress, or even panic in the worst cases. I get a serious case of sensory overload anytime I step into a Vegas casino, for example. How we distribute our focus and consciously process information coming from different sensory inputs is known as "attentional deployment." For ELVIS designers, this means being aware of how our experiencers are deploying their attention within our designs and being strategic in the number and sequence of senses we engage through our ELVIS designs.

It may mean reducing the number of senses engaged when focused attention on a task or challenge is needed, and increasing the number of senses engaged when we intend to broaden attention to a larger scope. Or, as in the intersectionality example, fewer senses may be engaged for more focused attention, but in a deeply immersive way. I like to think of this as the Spotlight-Floodlight design strategy.

The philosopher Alan Watts often spoke of our spotlight consciousness and our floodlight consciousness as two distinct ways of being in the world. Spotlight is intense and highly focused attentional deployment, and floodlight is expansive and illuminating attentional deployment. In terms of experience design, the spotlight strategy focuses experiencer attention by reducing the number of sensory inputs but maximizing their depth.

For example, think of a place where you prefer to do deep work—that is, work that requires your total attention to go deep on a task for a sustained amount of time. This is common for highly creative or intricate work such as problem solving, brain surgery, or even writing. In these times we do not want to multitask or become distracted by a lot of peripheral activity. We need to hone our conscious attentional spotlight on the objective before us. Our zone of awareness is very narrow and intense. In fact, to some degree we typically walk around with a kind of hazy spotlight consciousness in our daily lives, focusing mostly on what is right before us or just around the corner: the next meeting, the next task, the next thing on the schedule for the day.

On the other hand, sometimes we need to experience the world and ourselves through our floodlight consciousness. That means expanding our awareness and our sensory engagement to the fullest extent possible and synthesizing those inputs into the big picture and who we are, where we are, and what is going on around and within us.

A staple ingredient for immersion in most of my experience designs is meditation. There are many kinds of meditation, of course, but the one I use most frequently is known as "mindfulness meditation." However, it is a bit misnamed because this kind of meditation emphasizes calming down the usual calamity of our thinking minds—that is, quieting our intense and roaming spotlight consciousness and all the intellectual world of thoughts, words, symbols, and other filters through which we typically experience our lives. When we do this through practice, we discover another, hidden world underneath: our floodlight consciousness. In the floodlight, we deal with the raw and unfiltered experience of the world constantly flowing in through all of our senses, a tremendous source of experience that we have trained ourselves to ignore most of the time. The floodlight offers us a centered and holistic awareness of ourselves in the world.

For example, here is a simple somatic meditation to try. Right now as you read this sentence, take a deep breath. As you exhale, expand your attention to include the soles of your feet. What's going on down there? What surface are they touching? How does it feel? Is it rough? Smooth? Cold? Warm? Do you have shoes on? Socks maybe? Or are you barefoot? Are you comfy or in pain down there? And if you don't have feet, do this exercise with another mostly neglected body part.

Next, extrapolate from there upward and expand the meditation to more of your senses. Add one at a time until all your other senses are engaged toward a holistic "floodlight mind" where we "listen" with our entire bodies to the rich sensory experience available to us. Suddenly, even the experience of sitting in a chair reading a book is deepened and enriched. Living through your entire body is a self-centering experience and context-setting skill that we can encourage and

> Living through your entire body is a self-centering experience we can encourage and develop in our experience designs.

## Designer Tip

### *More Meditations*

There are many different meditation programs out there that you can tap into as a designer. Here are two very practical favorites of mine. The first is run by my lifelong friend, Bruce Moorman, called Mindful Meditation Australia. Their website (mindfulmeditationaustralia.org.au) includes exactly the kind of information and instructional routines an experience designer needs in order to get started, including daily intentions and goal mindfulness, self-check-ins, gratefulness meditations, full-presence practice in simple everyday activities, visualization and breathing sequences, and more. The second is AdaptiveYoga Specialist, run by Jennifer Jayanti Atkins, who focuses on immersive meditation and movement for people with neurodegenerative diseases and movement disorders (e.g., Parkinson's disease and traumatic brain injury). Her website includes classes, guided meditations and information on her research projects using fMRI brain scans during yogic practice (adaptiveyogaspecialist.com).

develop in our experience designs to make immersion personal. For designers, putting these two strategies together and employing both spotlight and floodlight modes in the course of an experience design is a powerful multisensory design strategy.

## Imaginative Immersion

How immersive an experience may be is not merely a function of how many senses it engages or how deeply, but also how effectively it synthesizes our sensory perceptions with our imaginations. For experience designers, this is done most powerfully through narrative. Each of the examples of immersive design mentioned above also includes a narrative element that makes it compelling, whether a theme park ride, a video game, or an interactive psychological exercise on intersectionality. When we become immersed in the narrative associated with the sensory inputs of an experience, fictional or real, the sensory inputs take on new and deeper meaning. This is known as "narrative transport," and it is a powerful design tool we need in our toolbox.

### Narrative Transport: A Vehicle for Immersion

Writers, artists, and entertainers are the world's grand storytellers. That's easy to see for dramatists such as novelists, film directors, screenwriters, actors, video game designers, and others who live and breathe stories. It is true of journalists and reporters as well, as they communicate world events to us through the stories they report on. It is also true for dancers, musicians, painters, and others whose work embodies an interpretation or expression of the human condition. And it is also true of leaders in all domains when they create narratives that inspire, motivate, and organize their charges to a higher purpose and excellence.

In all cases—from launching start-ups to leading transnational corporations, from articulating innovation challenges to bringing transformative products, services, and ideas to the people of the world, from guiding young people in parenting, education, or coaching to leading our own lives—when we are enraptured and imaginatively participate in compelling narratives that give us a sense of meaning, we become immersed in an experience.

Narrative transport refers to that magical moment when immersion happens. It is the crossing of the narrative threshold into a world of personal significance and larger meaning. In fictional scenarios, when a storyteller (writer or artist of any ilk) is successful in narrative transport, we the audience feel as though we are experiencing the events of the story ourselves or have somehow gotten lost in the story world, the performance, or the art. We may even lose awareness of our normal reality for a while.

Have you ever been reading a book on a sunny afternoon only to look up and surprisingly discover that several hours have slipped away unnoticed? Have you ever forgotten you were watching a movie or playing a video game until your phone suddenly lights up and buzzes, jerking you back to reality? Has music ever utterly overtaken your sense of time and space until it tragically comes to a conclusion and you are suddenly thrust back into your own skin?

In real-world scenarios, we experience narrative transport when we see ourselves within a larger story that provides purpose and direction, such as when a leader, coach, parent, or teacher frames our efforts into a compelling plot that drives us to do more than we thought we could. It occurs when we become invested in a narrative we see as so important, so attractive, or so full of passion that we want to become a part of it, contribute to it, help shape it. Without those narratives and the organizing and cohering effects they bring, morale falls, performance flounders, attrition increases. Especially in this era of COVID, making money at a job is not sufficient for our happiness. We crave a deeper sense of meaning in our lives.

As ELVIS designers, if our narrative design goals (whether fictional or real world) are successful, then we bring people into their discomfort zones in a way that impacts their sense of self. Narrative transport makes otherwise inaccessible experiences suddenly available to us. As a tool for ELVIS Experience Design Leadership, narrative transport can provoke experiencers to see the world and their relation to it anew. So how do we incorporate narrative transport into our ELVIS designs?

Research into this effect shows that the degree of narrative transportation people can experience—that is, how engaged with a narrative they become—depends on two critical factors:

- The level of empathy we are capable of feeling for the subjects of the narrative
- The number of connection points we perceive between the world of the narrative and our own lives—that is, our own identity narratives

For designers, this can be applied to our framing narrative for an experience—the story we present to experiencers as a launching pad for all that follows. The more universal connection points within an experience-framing narrative and the more relevant they are to our experiencers' own identity narratives, the more accessible the experience narrative is to their imaginations, the greater the degree of narrative transport, and the more imaginative immersion.

Keep in mind that universal themes of human experience (such as passion, struggle, pain, and inspiration) drive these feelings more than do specialized themes of any particular domain (such as expert knowledge, business jargon, or acronyms).

At the same time, we must balance making these connections with pushing our experiencers out of familiar territory and into personal discomfort zones where we know growth and change occur. We need to do both.

---

### Designer Tip

*Narrative Transport Design Guides*

1. **Establish a clear design point of view.** What do my leadership goals look like when considered through an experience design lens? What experiencer transformations and outcomes do I intend?

2. **Begin with the end in mind.** Describe the kind of experience narratives that might serve those goals and that you hope your experiencers may construct from your design. What elements will it include? What themes? What durable take-home elements that transfer beyond the design may result? Keep in mind that you will be inviting experiencers to cocreate their narratives with you rather than directing them from a position of power or authority, so you cannot foist a narrative on your experiencers. You invite them to it through the opportunities in your design. If you are designing strategic experiential opportunities for them, what narrative best unifies those opportunities, and what opportunities best support that narrative?

3. **Know your experiencers.** Consider the identity narratives of your experiencers and how they may or may not connect to the experience narrative you are shaping. In order to form multiple connection points to the narrative in your design, you will need to know something about their identity narratives. And here, more is better. If you are the leader of a team, you can likely delve quite deeply into the identity narratives of your experiencers. Specific tools for doing this are found in chapter 11. However, if you are designing experiences for the masses, such as a new product or service, an app, a book, or a theme park experience, you will have to make some broader assumptions about your audiences. Either way, as an experience designer, you will want to clearly delineate which elements of your narrative connect to your experiencers (thus facilitating narrative transport) and which push them into discomfort zones (thus facilitating growth), and then include opportunities for both.

4. **Transfer control.** Nothing supercharges narrative transport like experiencer ownership. One they have bought into a narrative and begin to help shape it, coauthor it, and make it their own, the immersion factor goes sky high. Therefore, the experience narrative you design for should be experiencer centered. That is, they are the living subject at the center of the experience. It is theirs. It is vitally important to frame and prime your experience narrative this way from the very beginning. Shifting the focus to a learner-centered approach unlocks the potential for experiencer control and agency through the lens of the story they are having their experience through, and the narrative they are forging as they do it. This equals narrative transport and immersion.

**Designer Tip**

*The Tools of Immersion*

One of the most powerful ELVIS tools for immersion is simply to consider the experience you are designing from a multisensory point of view and then go to work enhancing that angle. You may decide to apply some or all these tools as appropriate:

• Seek to increase the number and depth of the senses engaged in any experience component
• Use imaginative immersion and narrative transport strategies to enhance personal relevance
• Place your experiencers at the center and give them control over their immersion

## ELVIS Design Questions: Immersion

1. **Rate how much an experiencer may engage in the following sensory modalities in the design of the experience. (Note that your answers reflect what is intended or hoped for from the designer's perspective.)**

| | | | | | |
|---|---|---|---|---|---|
| Vision/Sight | 1 | 2 | 3 | 4 | 5 |
| Hearing | 1 | 2 | 3 | 4 | 5 |
| Taste | 1 | 2 | 3 | 4 | 5 |
| Touch | 1 | 2 | 3 | 4 | 5 |
| Smell | 1 | 2 | 3 | 4 | 5 |
| Kinesthetic sense | 1 | 2 | 3 | 4 | 5 |
| Imaginative | 1 | 2 | 3 | 4 | 5 |

Total for all questions: _____

ELVIS Zone (average score): _____

# 9 ■ Social and Emotional Involvement

Collaboration and Isolation Pathways to Greater
Experiential Depth and Discovery

*There is no blue without yellow and without orange.*

—Vincent Van Gogh

Social and emotional involvement is the next of the ELVIS 7 (see figure 14). In 2021, 90-year-old actor William Shatner, famous for his roles as Captain James T. Kirk in *Star Trek*, Denny Crane in *Boston Legal*, and many others, flew into space aboard a Blue Origin rocket. It was a short suborbital flight, but it afforded Shatner and his crewmates a stunning view of the Earth in all its grandeur and majesty from high above the atmosphere, not to mention the thrilling power and speed of the ascent, microgravity, and the journey back home. I've had the great privilege of speaking and communicating with Shatner on a number of occasions, even sharing the stage with him once to highlight the importance of environmental conservation and habitat protection, issues he is passionate about. But when I saw his tears and heard his emotional comments to his host,

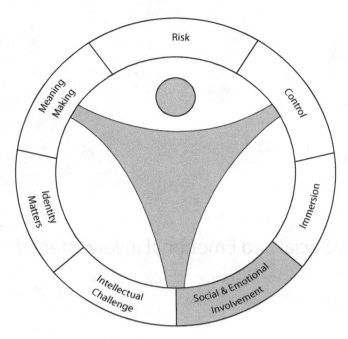

**Figure 14:** Social & Emotional Involvement

Jeff Bezos, moments after landing, I knew he'd had a transformative experience.

"I'm so filled with emotion about what just happened," he said. "It's extraordinary, extraordinary! I hope I can maintain what I feel now. I don't want to lose it. It's so much larger than me and life. What you have given me is the most profound experience I can imagine." After several months of bake time, he described the experience as inspiring a profound sense of urgently needing to protect our fragile home world. In his book *Boldly Go: Reflections on a Life of Awe and Wonder* (Variety, 2022), he passionately calls for action against climate change and habitat destruction in the face of mass extinctions and environmental degradation.

Beyond experience events and content, socioemotional elements are a huge aspect of transformative experience design and hugely unappreciated by leaders. Just as we discussed the importance of activating multiple senses within our ELVIS designs in the previous chapter, we also need to think about activating multiple emotions in our ELVIS designs here.

Note that I place social and emotional elements together because they so often co-occur and mutually reinforce each other. Social interactions among your team or group of experiencers have a tremendous influence on emotions. Our social interactions in any situation also have a large effect on both our sense of self and our sense of belonging (or exclusion), reflecting how validated and free we feel to express ourselves, and affecting our performance in any domain. For the ELVIS designer, this means incorporating group-based experiences of coming together, collaborating, and building empathy, respect, and a sense of belonging and social identity.

But nonsocial components are also important for ELVIS Experience Design Leadership. It is critical, for example, to include opportunities for solitary challenges in our experience designs that build personal identities and transfer control, permission, and ownership to individual experiencers. These components tap directly into those often-scary emotions of having to "go it alone." Good experience designs include both opportunities for social bonding with others and times of social separation or isolation for individuals. In this chapter we will examine how all this plays out in terms of emotional range and two phenomena critical to ELVIS designers: first with the Social Cohort Effect and then with the Solo Effect. But before we begin, we need to recognize the overall importance of the leader-experiencer relationship.

## What Is a Socioemotional Leader?

Among the many corporate teams that I work with, attending to socioemotional experiences via positive cohort effects and team cultural narratives often represents a significant departure from their existing notions of who leaders are and what leaders do.

For example, I often hear leaders spouting their trail-proven philosophies as bumper-sticker wisdom nuggets. And many of them sound pretty good on the surface. Maybe you've heard some of them:

> "I don't care how you feel or what you think; I only care about what you do and the quality of your work."
>
> "Focus on the task at hand. The rest will take care of itself."
>
> "I manage the process, not the people, and that keeps us all focused and equal."
>
> "You'll get a fair shake here. . . . I treat everyone the same regardless of their differences."
>
> "Bring your whole self to work, but check your 'issues' at the door."

Contrary to popular belief, such declarations are to me indicators of woefully inadequate leadership, ignorant of the underlying keys to success hiding in plain sight, that of the personal development of people and teams through the psychology of experiential design.

In many ways, command-and-control styles of leadership are easier and less ambiguous than alternative, often murkier, and certainly more difficult ideas of service leadership or distributed team leadership. And it is certainly not for everyone, for when you invite the psychology of performance, team cognition, and personal growth in, the floodgates of complexity, variability, and uncertainty slam open and you've got to have the mind-set and tools to deal with it.

When I present it, Experience Design Leadership using ELVIS is almost always seen as a radical departure from other leadership styles. Whereas most other leadership styles focus on a results-driven ethos alone, using the ELVIS Framework and Toolkit places the emphasis on the experiences of people and teams. That is, the experiential process itself becomes a product and a metric of success. The results are the individual and collective narratives of the experience, and any additional results in terms of outputs (products or services they create, inventions, athletic performance, achievement of group or personal goals, etc.) are seen as parts of that experience narrative.

The ultimate questions that are posed to teams in ELVIS Experience Design Leadership are, What are we doing? Why and how are we doing it? and Who are we becoming as we do it? If the answers do not resonate with personal relevance, a

The ultimate questions in ELVIS Experience Design Leadership are, What are we doing? Why and how are we doing it? and Who are we becoming as we do it?

degree of risk and discomfort, and the possibility of identity growth, then I would observe that a cohort leadership opportunity has been missed.

## Emotional Kaleidoscopes in Experience Design

There is often a presumption among leaders that we need to keep everyone in our groups or teams happy and feeling good at all times in order for an experience to be "successful." For ELVIS Experience Design Leadership, however, this could not be further from the truth. Our experiencers are not in vacation mode, and we, as designers and leaders, are not their servers. In fact, we should expect our experiencers to have multiple emotional reactions to good ELVIS designs, and we should not shy away from them. They are necessary for growth and exploration, integral precursors to transformative experiences. So bring on the emotional kaleidoscope.

We should expect multiple emotional reactions to good ELVIS designs and we should not shy away from them.

Critically, experience designers need to recognize that there is no "clean slate" going in to any given experience. Experiencers walk through the door carrying with them an entire emotional landscape upon which they are located—positive, negative, and every imaginable state in between. Whatever you've designed is already modified by the variety of emotional states and points of view of your experiencers.

But rather than being a threat to your design, the challenge is to make this into a feature. One of the hallmarks of a good ELVIS design is that it evokes multiple emotional experiences that may include

nervous anticipation and anxiety, thrill and elation, sometimes dis-
appointment or regret, revelation, and more. Knowing that the
emotional components of the experience you've designed are closely
tied to personal relevance and risk perceptions of experiencers (as we
have already explored), the task becomes one of tailoring the design
to the preexisting emotional status of experiencers so they can be
emotionally challenged, provoked, and inspired. How do we do that?
It begins with personal dialogue.

Like you, I've had experiencers enter with all kinds of emotional
preamble: people going through divorce and custody battles, people
struggling with illness or the illness of loved ones, people celebrat-
ing success and abundance, people striving to prove themselves,
people grieving lost loved ones or lost life pathways, people hoping
for a renewal or rebirth or passage out of their current identities. But
I would not know about any of that if I did not do three things:

• Ask about experiencers' life circumstances
• Ask early
• Work to establish a trust rapport for a genuine conversa-
  tion to happen

The relationship between leader and team member, mentor and protégé, teacher and student, parent and child, coach and athlete, consultant and client, designer and experiencers is where this emotional
connection must begin, and mutual vulnerability is at its heart. Expressing a genuine curiosity about your experiencers' perceptions,
self-reflections, aspirations, and concerns is the first step. Becoming
vulnerable and sharing your own stories and perceptions is the second.
Signaling that you are engaged in a mutual journey and will be sharing the experience to come from differing points of view is the third.

The time, opportunity, and mind-set for building this kind of personal relationship must be part of your experience design. And
while the initial conversations should ideally begin in the pre-
experience phase, you will likely find, as I have, the important elements of experiencers' personal stories are often only revealed later
on within the frame of discomfort zone experiences, indicating the
need for continuing dialogue with your experiencers as a design strategy during the experience and post-experience phases.

**Designer Tip**

*Social-Emotional Continuum*

Keep in mind that social-emotional factors exist along a continuum from positive to negative. You need to be aware of how the experience is emotionally landing with your experiencers by asking the following questions:

- How are you feeling about this [experience component]?
- What are you positively anticipating or hoping for? What would be the best outcome for you emotionally?
- What are you concerned about or hoping to avoid? How would you feel in that case?
- How do your social interactions with others affect your emotions on this?

And later . . .

- How did you feel about that [experience component]?
- What were the pros and cons for you emotionally?
- What has been the social impact of others on your experience and on how you feel about yourself?

Sharing your own past experiences or feelings about the current one is a good way to establish rapport for these discussions. Designers who attend to this important aspect through dialogue with their experiencers and then design components that intentionally activate multiple emotions are usually rewarded with many undesigned and emergent positive outcomes, such as the following:

- Group encouragement and support in challenging moments of an experience
- Shared joy and celebration in the wake of positive experiences
- Resilience in the face of hardship or tragedy
- Lifelong friendships forming among the group

For designers who ignore this aspect, they often find themselves in salvage mode, trying to rescue an experience from disaster, and scratching their heads about what went wrong.

Beyond these dialogues, we designers must then respond by tweaking our designs. This means identifying their social-emotional discomfort zones and then creating or amplifying opportunities to safely enter those discomfort zones, inviting them to grow in those directions.

## Kuleana and the Social Cohort Effect

For years I've designed and delivered transformative leadership experiences for corporate executives from dozens of companies, and personal transformation experiences for teens (most recently through a program I created for the Bayer Corporation, the Bayer International Teen Science Camp). For the teens, these experiences involved intense physical, emotional, and intellectual challenges, very often in the wilds of high and remote mountains. For the execs, while sometimes they too opted for that level of adventure, it was more common to occur within their very own boardrooms or (thanks to COVID) videoconference rooms and involve explorations of identity, race, gender, personal meaning, and leadership. Throughout this work, I've been privileged to explore many surprising commonalities between these two groups and how their transformative experiences often pivot around a tension between individual and social elements.

Of course, there are some big differences between these two groups worth noting. No matter what country they come from, the teens are "greener." They are more raw and unsure, more innocent, less confident (despite what their outward demeanor may sometimes indicate), but also much more honest. In most ways that matter, they are closer to the frontiers of their lives.

The corporate executives, on the other hand, are more shielded from the harsher edges of their lives. They have crafted personal buffers through the hard bark of experience, status, and the isolating remoteness that importance often brings. But beneath that hard bark are the inner tree rings of their personal identities—the still-tender living sapwood of their essential being and the not-forgotten childlike wonder of their central heartwood. This is where the two groups are very much the same. And this is precisely from where their transformative experiences emerge, where innocence in the face of the unknown must invite in what is new.

My opening lines to establish the experience narrative when first gathering a new group of execs or teens in these programs are almost the same for both groups. I say something like this:

> *Look around you. Look at the strangers sitting next to you, across from you, looking back at you. You don't know them and they don't know you. Two weeks from now, I guarantee you, there will be tears at your parting. There will be tight embraces. There will be long last looks and haunting intuitions about the fleeting moments of life, as you bid each other farewell.*

They never believe me.

They laugh uncomfortably and move on with the niceties and manners of meeting and greeting one another in cordial and refined ways (yes, even the teenagers). But I continue with the comments I will invariably echo several weeks hence, on the eve of our departure from one another:

> *Here we are, together, in this time and this place. As a group of new friends and colleagues, we will never be here again, not like this. Never again will we assemble to do the things we will do here together—the risks we will take, the adventures we will share, the experiences we will build. Oh, you might have reunions as time marches on, almost all groups do. But this moment together, this time of our lives here and now, will never come again. Seize it. Take a chance. Expand yourself. It is, after all, your experience. How will you choose to live it?*

I say these things to call attention to the threshold on which they stand, one that is both powerfully individual and intimately social in nature. For it is not only an individual experience but also a group experience that includes the people on the journey alongside them who will, without exception, play a huge role in sharing and shaping what transpires. In sociology, this is related to social construction, collaborative learning, and social learning theory, where experiences are molded into meaning in concert with other people.

The experiences are carefully customized and two or three weeks in duration, intended to push their limits, expand their capacities, and challenge their sense of self. These are transformative experiences by design, and the perspective I lend with my little speech is actually a narrative frame (framing and priming again) through which they can activate their own transformations individually and socially. In truth, the same speech could be given about any opportunities in our lives for personal "stretch assignments" that also demand close social interaction. These are chances for experiencing ourselves and others in new and undiscovered ways. I call this the "Social Cohort Effect."

The Social Cohort Effect for any given group and any given experience grows with time as the designed experience progresses. It typically follows a pattern important for designers to know, from an assembly of strangers with their individual identities to a group of colleagues who develop a common social identity. When transformative experiences occur, they can progress to a sense of family that can last for years.

As ELVIS designers, we can facilitate this pattern by encouraging thought and shared reflection about their experiences on three nested levels:

- From the perspective of their personal identities
- As group members forging a new social identity
- As different people meeting significant challenges together through risk taking

I observed this effect powerfully in Hawaii, where I first encountered the concept of *Kuleana*. I later began to design for it in every experience, as I describe below.

### What Is Kuleana?

During my dissertation, I was privileged to research a group of educators on a strenuous science learning journey in the remote wilds of the Hawaiian Islands, which I mentioned briefly in chapter 6. I observed as they transformed from a group of strangers to an intimate and mutually supportive band of colleagues with a responsibility to one another, much in the vein of the Hawaiian concept of Kuleana, as described by our Hawaiian hosts and my adviser at the time, Mike Marlow.

Kuleana is a wonderful concept, referring to a deep sense of reciprocal responsibility and the relationship between the one responsible and the thing they are responsible for. For example, in Hawaiian culture, the people have Kuleana to the land, a responsibility to respect and protect it. The land, in turn, feeds and shelters the people. Kuleana to other people is like an extended sense of family, where members mutually care for, respect, and protect one another.

> Kuleana refers to a deep sense of reciprocal responsibility and the relationship between the one responsible and the thing they are responsible for.

This group of teachers faced numerous challenges designed into the experience, including strenuous hikes over sharp and treacherous lava fields, deep into lava tubes, and high up on the volcanoes of the islands; exploration of inland rivers and river deltas by kayak; difficult sample collection near active lava flows; picture assays while snorkeling the coral reefs; night diving with manta rays; and even scuba diving with sharks. The risk invitations were designed to be faced as a group, where members could mutually support each other in the various risk decisions each person made. It was not without drama and disagreement. It was not without touching displays of compassion and empathy.

As their sense of Kuleana grew over the weeks, the teachers forged a common social identity as members of a community, in addition to being individuals on a journey. This cohort effect spilled over most notably in their nested reflections on their own identities as educators, as group members, and as people who could rise to new challenges they hadn't thought themselves capable of before.

The same thing often occurs within the designed experiences my team at NCWIT and I create for corporate leaders. We design leadership experiences for them to learn the social science of group dynamics and team cognition in order to create more innovative, inclusive, and effective team cultures (discussed in the next section). Just as with the teachers, the Social Cohort Effect pattern is anchored on the participants' nested reflections on their own identities as leaders, as members of a team of leaders, and as people rising to new and unexpected challenges together. When the positive cohort effect takes hold, we see a mutually supportive yet mutually challenging culture of growth and change emerge.

> When a positive cohort effect takes hold, we see a mutually supportive yet mutually challenging culture emerge.

Positive cohort effects and Kuleana align with the benefits research has demonstrated for social and collaborative learning, including increased inquiry and knowledge gains through social dialogue and discovery, increased retention of what is learned, greater group bonding, and collaborative problem solving. Social learning

## Designer Tip

### *Designing for Positive Cohort Effects*

For ELVIS designers, it is well worth it to attend to the formation of a positive cohort effect as a group evolves through a common challenge. This refers to providing a structured means for them to reflect on and make meaning from their group experiences on several levels:

- At their individual identity level
- At their social identity level (membership in the group, team, or community with responsibility to others)
- As people taking personal risks together to rise to challenges that are hard and for which they have a low sense of agency

Do this by explicitly prompting for these levels of reflection within discussions, group meetings, journaling, or other forms of structured meaning making during the experience (for more examples, see chapter 12). When so attended to, the cohort effect for a given designed experience is a powerful positive influence for participants.

has also been linked to better employee motivation, knowledge, morale, inclusion, and retention.

### Social Cohorts and Team Cultures

The cohort effect in team dynamics is revealed through team culture. In my work on corporate culture construction at the National Center for Women and IT (NCWIT), my team uses the following definition of team culture:

> *A defining set of shared norms and values, processes, and practices influencing how group members interact, work together, solve problems, support one another, and face new experiences.*

Culture is dynamically created every day, as opposed to being something that is set once and solidified ever after. Individual actions and team cultural dynamics mutually create each other; they are reciprocal. Team culture determines what kinds of individual behaviors are acceptable and desirable. Collectively, interactions among team members continually create and re-create the culture.

Think of a team you are a part of as leader or as a member. If you ask each member what the team's norms and values are, do you think they will give the same answer? If you ask them what the team's identity narrative is, how much will they agree? Will they even know what you mean by that? If the leader has conducted explicit discussions or activities to intentionally attend to team culture, then you might very well see some congruence on how the members describe it. Such teams usually have a tight sense of purpose, coordination, and inclusion for their members. This is a positive team cohort effect.

But if a team has not made an effort to visibly define its own culture and invite members to contribute to it, then the usual result is that each member has widely differing views and experiences of the team's culture, often at odds with each other or in direct conflict. This inhibits performance, problem solving, and the quality of each individual's experiences on that team.

This is especially true for marginalized group members, whether because of race, ethnicity, gender, age, ability, or intersections of all these. Such team members feel greater pressures to conform to the team's cultural norms in order to "fit in" rather than be authentic to their own intersectional selves and try to shape the team's cultural norms, at the risk of their sense of belongingness on the team (as shallow as that belonging might be).

A team's culture is, of course, greatly influenced by the leader. When we adopt an ELVIS Experience Design Leadership stance, the team's cohort effect and culture are now seen to be governed by the team's identity narrative, as created and shared by its members. The challenge then is to nurture team cultural narratives that are large and complex enough to include all team members yet unifying enough to ground a collective team identity.

One of the most powerful tools for an experience design leader is to guide the formation of just such a shared narrative and keep it foregrounded over time, which is not easy. Team identity narratives change just as individual identity narratives change, and many times much faster. Drivers of this change include changes in leadership and membership, new challenges the team must face, and changing circumstances and the larger context in which the team must operate.

So as ELVIS Experience Design Leaders, we must recognize these changes and facilitate the ongoing creation of team identity narratives that set the stage for the kind of social-emotional involvement needed for high-performing and inclusive teams. If we are especially skilled, it also sets the stage for transformative experiences.

## Designer Tip

### *Setting the Socioemotional Stage*

- **Create a vision:** Establish clear and elevating goals that people can believe in and personally own.
- **Promote mutuality:** Express the idea that we are all different but we are all interdependent. Our culture and our experiences together are what we

make of them. This is the opposite of being mutually competitive but does not negate challenging each other.

- **Share control:** Distribute power and responsibility. This does not mean abdicating your leadership responsibilities. To the contrary, it is a form of team leadership that demands a developmental approach as opposed to a blunt command-and-control style of leadership.
- **Use participatory design:** Whenever possible, invite team members to contribute to the shaping of their experiences together, a component of both "communities of practice" and "team leadership theory." This means collaboration in many forms and the expectation of cocreative and mutually supportive action from group members.
- **Advance the team identity narrative:** Attend to the launch and evolution of the team identity narrative as opportunities emerge, events occur, and membership changes. This includes framing successes and failures toward the growth of the team's collective identity.

## The Solo Effect: Agency Building by Going It Alone

The legendary outdoor program Outward Bound has a wonderful designed experience—the solo overnight. My good friend Pablo, who used to run Outward Bound experiences for several years, describes it as an opportunity for kids (or adults) to camp out on their own, far away from sight and sound of anyone else, alone in the wilderness, for at least one overnight. It's a simple enough design but represents a huge challenge for many people. If you have not tried this or something similar, it is hard to describe the experience of removing your social safety net and "going it alone" in the face of uncertainty. It is directly aimed at inviting people into their discomfort zones. Now a high school educator and teacher trainer, Pablo the Educator uses similar strategies to invite people to solo experiences.

In my own work, I look for ways to present solo risk invitations to my experiencers. For corporate executives working with my team at NCWIT, we challenge them to become inclusive culture construction ambassadors, facing large groups of their direct reports and colleagues to lead discussions about inclusivity and diversity, a topic usually well outside their expertise. For my international teen programs, I challenge them to splinter off from the group for a solo hike in the high mountains of Colorado with no one else around, conjuring fears of bears and mountain lions for many of them, or just the fear of not being able to navigate back to the group. For aspiring professionals hoping to advance their careers, I challenge them to create stretch assignments for themselves that isolate them from their teams but encourage them to seek out new personal mentors and sponsors to help them on their journeys.

In all cases, the challenges and benefits of "going solo" represent a special category of risk: isolation. A large part of the risk we perceive is the disappearance of the cohort. Even if you happen to be a self-proclaimed introvert (like me) or have a number of positive experiences going it alone, there is something unique in the kinds of risk we engage in when we go solo. Beyond the obvious loss of others to rely on should something go wrong, there is the disappearance of our social audience, real or imagined. In terms of identity development, as we discussed in chapter 4, when we are isolated from the cohort, we quiet our social identities and lose a sense of our reflected self-appraisals (that is, what we think others are thinking of us). This effect increases as time alone is increased, until we are left with only our self-appraisals. It's just me, myself, and the wall, so to speak. Our personal identities rise to the occasion.

Think of a time you had to go it alone, whether alone among a group of strangers or alone with no one else in sight. It might be the first time you rode a bike or drove a car without anyone else present. It might be a long journey you undertook alone. It might be your first solo flight as a pilot in training, in which you and you alone would have to land the plane in the absence of your instructor. It might be moving to a new place where you knew no one. Maybe it was a presentation you had to make alone in the spotlight, or a mission you were sent on. It might be becoming an empty nester. It could be the loss of a partner or parent or child. How did you feel? What was going through your mind? What were the risks you could identify? What was your interpretation of it later on? The feelings associated with going solo range from thrilling to validating to terrifying to heartbreaking. Sometimes the anxiety and stress of going it alone appear only within the relief we feel when the risk experience passes.

The importance of having experiences where we "go it alone" resides within agency development. It increases our confidence and capacity for taking on risks inside our discomfort zones and being able to do more than we thought we could. As we explored in chapter 4, often the risk decision is more important than the risk outcome for developing the sense of agency. Whether we succeed or fail (provided we fail forward), or achieve something in between, a heightened sense of accomplishment comes with such experiences. Doing something brave requires courage. Courage can only emerge from a place of vulnerability. Solo vulnerability is a special flavor of vulnerability, facing the anxiety, thrill, and intrigue of discovering and pushing your own limits in isolation. It is also of owning a sense of adventure and engaging in something difficult and exciting. All these emotions tied to solo components of a designed experience can serve to amplify one's sense of agency, pride, and self-efficacy. And it is worth noting that experiencers' prior emotional states going in, as well as any fear and anxiety about particular risk decisions they face, are critical. Without these pre-emotions, the experience of solo risk taking would have little or no meaning.

> Courage can only come from a place of vulnerability. Solo vulnerability is a special flavor of vulnerability.

For designers, solo experiences are critical for increasing the potential for people to have transformative experiences. Weaving solo risk invitations in with positive social cohort experiences is a winning combination. Not everyone will accept solo risk invitations. Sometimes it results in regret. Sometimes accepted risk invitations result in failure, whereupon you must be ready with your strategies for failing forward. But solo components in our designed experiences grant us the opportunity we rarely give ourselves permission to engage in—facing the world on our own terms, in our own way, and dropping all pretenses and masks of our other performed identities. We then fully occupy and live deeply through our personal identities as conscious beings in the place we call here and the time we call now. It is an experience of being fully alive.

**Designer Tip**

*Social and Emotional Design Guides*

Combining the above material into practical use, here are easy-to-implement design guides for social and emotional involvement:

- Conduct frequent check-ins: Design for both group and individual check-ins during all three phases: pre-experience, experience, and post-experience.
- Build in reflection and gut-check journaling: Design for one or more methods for experiencers to contemplate and then record their social and emotional involvement. These include old-fashioned pen-and-paper journals, blogs, online groups and forums, and videos. For examples of narrative tools, see chapter 12.
- Design for both group and solo components of the experience if possible.
- Design for components that partners or small groups must face together. This could include collaborative tasks, partner activities, or group challenges.
- Use collaborative narrative construction strategies. This could include such things as personal documentary video creation in pairs or groups, co-journaling, or shared responsibilities for facilitating group discussions.
- Use frustration-value maps periodically as a discussion focus. This is where each experiencer makes two columns on paper: one listing their current frustrations (negative) and the other listing the values they hold that have been violated owing to the frustration (positive). For example, I might list a frustration that no one listens to me or takes me seriously, reflecting a value that I believe everyone should have a voice and be respected. This tool is especially useful if you detect a negative cohort effect is happening.
- Incorporate socioemotional elements such as the Four "F" Factors:
  - Fun Factor: Ensure elements of your designed experience are fun from your experiencers' points of view.
  - Fear Factor: Ensure that your design has some element of risk, uncertainty, and discomfort, again from your experiencers' points of view.

○ Feeling Factor: Ensure that your design includes opportunities for both touching the emotions and expressing and sharing them among your cohort.

○ Friendship Factor: Design for multiple opportunities for people to forge friendships. Often this includes setting a friendly context of supportive colleagues and providing unstructured downtime combined with the collaborative elements mentioned above.

## ELVIS Design Questions: Social and Emotional Involvement

1. **How would you describe the overall ratio of group-based versus individual or independent experiences in the design? (Note: The most common metric for this is the amount of time experiencers will spend in each kind of experience.)**
   ○ Entirely group based (100%)
   ○ Mostly group based (75%)
   ○ Equally group based and independent (50/50%)
   ○ Mostly independent (75%)
   ○ Entirely independent (100%)

2. **For the group-based experiences, please indicate how much an experiencer may engage in the following emotional dynamics in the design of the experience:**

| | | | | | |
|---|---|---|---|---|---|
| Sense of group-belonging | 1 | 2 | 3 | 4 | 5 |
| Collaboration | 1 | 2 | 3 | 4 | 5 |
| Empathy & compassion for others | 1 | 2 | 3 | 4 | 5 |
| Mutual respect | 1 | 2 | 3 | 4 | 5 |
| Observation, imitation, modeling | 1 | 2 | 3 | 4 | 5 |
| Fear and uncertainty | 1 | 2 | 3 | 4 | 5 |

3. **For the individual or independent experiences, please indicate how much an experiencer may engage in the following emotional dynamics in the design of the experience:**

| | | | | | |
|---|---|---|---|---|---|
| Feelings of independence (including excitement and/or anxiety) | 1 | 2 | 3 | 4 | 5 |
| Self-reliance | 1 | 2 | 3 | 4 | 5 |
| Courage in response to challenges | 1 | 2 | 3 | 4 | 5 |
| Resilience in response to failures | 1 | 2 | 3 | 4 | 5 |
| Personal accomplishment | 1 | 2 | 3 | 4 | 5 |
| Fear and uncertainty | 1 | 2 | 3 | 4 | 5 |

Total for all questions: _____
ELVIS Zone (average score): _____

Weighted Scoring Option:
Use this option to very roughly accommodate experience designs falling on either extreme of group based or independent.

- If your experience is mostly or entirely group based, multiply your answer to question 2 by 1.5 or 2.0, respectively.
- Conversely, if your experience is mostly or entirely independent, multiply your answer to question 3 by 1.5 or 2.0, respectively.

# 10 ▪ Intellectual Challenge

Activating Curiosity and Problem Solving

*Life is an unfoldment, and the further we travel the more truth we can comprehend. To understand the things that are at our door is the best preparation for understanding those that lie beyond.*

—Hypatia,
Greek mathematician, philosopher

*But as for me, I am tormented with an everlasting itch for things remote. I love to sail forbidden seas, and land on barbarous coasts.*

—Herman Melville,
*Moby Dick*

Intellectual challenges, learning new things about the world and ourselves, and expanding one's knowledge in the process have consistently emerged in my work as critical experiential variables and indicators for transformative experiences (see figure 15). For many of you, leaders of innovation in particular, intellectual challenge is

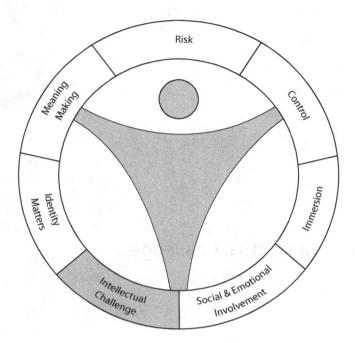

**Figure 15:** Intellectual Challenge

already built in to what you do. It's part of the DNA of why your cohorts and teams and organizations exist. My hope here is to build on your existing knowledge by offering a new perspective on intellectual challenges and some design tools to unlock their transformative potential in concert with the other ELVIS tools.

We have defined transformative experiences as learning experiences that can and should operate on several levels in your experience designs. Just like intellectual challenge everywhere, intellectual challenge in experience designs comes in the forms of innovation, exploration, discovery, and, most powerfully, problem solving. In the best experience designs, intellectual challenges are embedded within all three design phases: pre-experience, experience, and post-experience. And intellectual challenges are certainly linked to risk invitations and risk decisions. Experiences that lack intellectual engagement are often reported to be boring, not challenging (despite aspects of physical or social challenge), or not as significant as other experiences. To understand why, let's take a closer look at intellectual challenges and how to apply them within the Experiential Learning Variables & Indicators System.

### How to Build Narrative Grounding for Intellectual Challenges: Linking Learning with Identity

In the *Timaeus* (360 BCE), one of the very first works on natural philosophy, Plato writes about the transformative nature of knowledge, declaring that knowledge changes the knower. He claims that our choice of study provides pathways out of confusion and disharmony. It is a notion echoed down through the ages to everyone who has felt the thirst for discovery and experienced personal growth as a result of quenching that thirst.

Yet rooting that thirst for knowledge within identity narratives that articulate a reason behind our intellectual engagement is something we mostly shy away from in traditional leadership, education and parenting paradigms. But it is exactly where we must go for transformative experience design.

Such grounding narratives must be powerful enough to speak to us of our origins, our future, our ideals, our conduct, and above all our purpose here and now. In short, they must be identity narratives credible and complex enough to root our intellectual engagement deeply within ourselves for any given experience. To do so places the experiencer—the learner—in context with what is being learned, thereby establishing personal relevance and personal meaning.

Thus, it is not enough to simply throw intellectual challenges and problem solving into our experience designs. As designers, if we can tie intellectual challenges to our experiencers' process of deeply examining and potentially altering their own identity narratives, then we are effectively inviting them to a conversation that holds the possibility of transformation. As I like to say in my workshops, when properly narrated, learning equals identity development.

> When properly narrated, learning equals identity development.

How do we set up this kind of narrative grounding for intellectual challenge in our ELVIS designs? We tackle it head on through explicit narrative construction.

### Step 1: Set Your Own Stance for Intellectual Challenge

Begin with your own philosophical stance and the narrative behind the intellectual challenges in your design:

- What is my overall perspective on learning and intellectual challenge?
- Why am I including certain challenges in this design? How do they serve my larger goals?
- How and when are intellectual challenges embedded in the experience? Be specific.
- How do the intellectual challenges complement and/or blend with other ELVIS design elements? They should not be isolated but rather integrated.
- What flexibility exists to accommodate my experiencers' views and capabilities regarding intellectual challenges? (Are there possibilities to customize, either by the designer or by the experiencer?)
- How will I know if the intellectual challenges I designed are working? (What metrics or observations would they include? Examples: successful solutions to problems, level of engagement, time on task, levels of collaboration, frustration, enthusiasm, effects on the cohort, individual reactions through interviews, impacts on self-esteem.)

### Step 2: Link Learning to Experiencer Identity

Expand the discussion with your experiencers using the following prompts to start the process of linking learning with their identity narratives. They can be used with individuals or groups via discussions, journaling, blogging, podcasting, video creation, and more.

- What intellectual challenges exist in your life right now?

- How would you describe your relationship to intellectual challenges and learning? How do you tackle them?
- What kinds of intellectual challenges are you most and least comfortable with? Why?
- What invitations are you making for new learning in your life (now and in the future)?

*Step 3: Generate Grounding Narratives for Intellectual Challenge*

This is the explicit creation of personal narratives that integrate the intellectual challenges of your designed experience. It can be done with individuals and/or groups. It can include shared narratives or individual ones that differ. Many times, comparing differing grounding narratives deepens the experience. Finally, this can be done at several times during an experience, initially to set the stage but also periodically to check in with your experiencers and keep it top-of-mind for them as needed. Aim for the following narrative components:

- A clear and elevating goal
- An articulation of the reasons you are engaged in this experience and its intellectual challenges, including what experiencers bring to the learning and what they hope to come away with
- How the intellectual challenges complement or merge with other experience elements (the ELVIS 7)

Examples of such narrative grounding, old and new, are all around. For Edison's Menlo Park team it was the electric light that would change us into a wired society. For *Apollo* it was a mission to the moon that would change us into a spacefaring people. For Industrial Light and Magic it was the invention of art and technologies that would change moviemaking forever. For the Tesla car company it was the dream of an electric car and its batteries that would begin to break our reliance on fossil fuels. And those are just inventions. Examples also include ideas and problem solving: the Copernican revolution of a sun-centered solar system, democracy's evolution from various native cultures and the ancient Greeks to today, feminism, civil rights, the internet—all intellectual leaps forward rooted in narratives that give personal meaning and shared purpose.

So once narratively grounded, how do we best implement intellectual challenges into our experience designs? We employ what I call Experiential Inquiry-Based Design.

### What Is Experiential Inquiry-Based Design?

Several years ago, I hosted a conference on transformative experiences in science learning. It actually followed an "un-conference" model because rather than forcing the 400-plus participants to sit through hours of PowerPoint parades (as all too common at conferences), I had set up micro-experiences for participants to choose from. Each experience was designed using ELVIS and included intellectual challenges using experiential learning theory and inquiry-based learning. The only mandate to participants was to choose experiences that in some way represented their discomfort zones. Here's what was on the menu:

Science of yoga

Scuba diving

Physics of indoor skydiving

Lego EV3 robotics

Physiology with an altitude

Anatomy in clay

GeoSpatial orienteering

Solar rollers

Jane Goodall's community mapping

Wilderness survival

Digital nature stories and cell phone photography

Indoor and outdoor rock climbing

Mobile apps development

Wolf behavior camp

Hydrobot construction

Whispering horses

GoPro paragliding

Zip line engineering

GoPro paddle boarding

Wilderness map and compass

Raft the Rockies

Star party astronomy

After each day's events, we would conduct evening fireside chats to discuss and unpack the experiences through the ELVIS lens, peeking behind the design curtain for each experience. Among the design perspectives we explored was Experiential Inquiry-Based Learning. Experiential learning has taken on many disguises over the years: hands-on learning, minds-on learning, service learning, discovery learning, problem-based learning, project-based learning, and more. I like elements of each of these. They all involve direct, first-person engagement. As Confucius is credited with saying (who knows if he actually did),

> *Tell me and I will forget. Show me and I may remember.*
> *Involve me and I will understand.*

My translation: experience is the difference between knowledge and understanding. You can tell a person about the water temperature and flow rate during spring runoff season, and

> Experience is the difference between knowledge and understanding.

they will *know* something about the river. But not until they feel the rush of the water carrying them over rapids and rocks with spray in their face and the roar of the water in their ears will they *understand* the river.

A hallmark of experiential learning is the outward appearance of chaos. Rather than highly directed and coordinated activity, it is messy, individualized, and variable. Think of it as the difference between an orchestrated classical concert and an improvisational jazz festival. For the Experience Design Leader this is not to be feared; it is to be welcomed. It indicates an experiencer-centered and experiencer-directed design. Traditional training and learning methods are content centered. They focus on the content and what is to be learned rather than on the experiencer and the experience of learning. In experiential learning, leaders are "guides on the sides" rather than "sages on stages."

Another hallmark of Experiential Inquiry-Based Learning is that it is driven by questions. These usually come in the form of problems to be solved. Inquiry sparks a sequential process that is outlined in the Designer Tip below. Sometimes you can follow only part of this sequence in your ELVIS designs owing to other constraints. But it is good to design for the entire sequence and to make it transparent to your experiencers.

---

**Designer Tip**

*Experiential Inquiry Design Flow*

A design flow I use for intellectual challenges follows a sequence that looks like this:

1. **Make the inquiry:** A question is posed or a problem is articulated. This includes the overall context, topic, or field of the inquiry combined with specifics about the question or problem to be solved.
2. **Conduct ideation:** Possible answers or solutions are brainstormed and discussed for viability.
3. **Identify knowledge needed:** Experiencers identify what knowledge, skills, or data they need to acquire to address the inquiry based on their ideation. They may revisit this if none of their ideas turn out to be viable.
4. **Investigate:** Gather the needed knowledge, whether by observations, research, experiments or tests, or other means.
5. **Apply:** Apply the knowledge earned to the question or problem to see if it answers it or solves the problem or at least sheds light on it.
6. **Reflect:** Assess what was learned from different perspectives and make meaning.

\* **Capture Affective Reactions:** Embedded within each step, experiencers record and/or discuss their learning experience, how and what they are thinking and why, and how they are feeling, and identify what risks they are taking, what gains they are making, and what improvements in the experience they desire.

**ELVIS Design Questions: Intellectual Challenge**

1. **How would you describe the extent to which experiencers have a narrative grounding that overlaps with their identity narratives for the intellectual challenges in the experience?**
   1. There is no narrative grounding for intellectual challenges, and identity narratives are not considered.
   2. Narrative grounding for intellectual challenges is left to the experiencers to establish if they care to.
   3. Narrative grounding for intellectual challenges is loosely established but without experiencer identity narratives integrated into their design.
   4. Intellectual challenges are grounded in narratives that overlap with experiencers' identity narratives to some extent.
   5. The intellectual challenges are designed with experiencer identity narratives in mind and are customized for their growth in collaboration with experiencers.

2. **How would you describe the way intellectual challenges (including new knowledge and/or skills development) are encountered by experiencers in your design?**
   1. Content, knowledge, and/or skills are transmitted one way, from leader, educator, parent, or coach to the experiencers. Experiencers are expected to absorb and understand on their own.
   2. Content, knowledge, and/or skills are transmitted from leader, educator, parent, or coach to the experiencers. Experiencers are expected to absorb and understand, but with some supports or structured interactions with the leader designed into the experience to facilitate understanding.
   3. Experiencers are introduced to content, knowledge, and/or skills by the leader, educator, parent, or coach but equally share responsibility with the leader for comprehension and synthesis with prior understanding.

4. Experiencers encounter content, knowledge, and/or skills in discovery mode in response to a challenge, project, or problem articulated by the leader, educator, parent, or coach. Their comprehension, synthesis, and application of the new learning are supported with structured interactions between the leader and experiencer peers (if group based).

5. Experiencers encounter content, knowledge, and/or skills in discovery mode in response to a challenge, project, or problem that they themselves define and articulate. Comprehension, synthesis, and application of the new learning are experiencer driven and directed (and shared among experiencer peers if group based). The leader, educator, parent, or coach role is to support and encourage as needed to facilitate an experiencer-directed experience.

3. **To what extent does the design allow for opportunities for the following intellectual experiences?**

| | | | | | |
|---|---|---|---|---|---|
| Application of new and existing knowledge to new situations | 1 | 2 | 3 | 4 | 5 |
| Curiosity and wonder | 1 | 2 | 3 | 4 | 5 |
| Skepticism | 1 | 2 | 3 | 4 | 5 |
| Problem solving (including problem defining, ideation, cognitive flexibility, and experimentation) | 1 | 2 | 3 | 4 | 5 |

Total for all questions: _____

ELVIS Zone (average score): _____

# 11 ■ Identity Matters

Integrating Our Uniqueness and Avoiding One-Size-Fits-All Traps

*If you are always trying to be normal, you will never know how amazing you can be.*

—Maya Angelou

*You went to somewhere to do something with an anticipated goal in mind, something you couldn't do elsewhere and be the same Self.*

—Jerome Bruner,
*Acts of Meaning*

Identity matters, as we explored in chapter 4, are foundational to the ELVIS Framework. Now it's time to examine identity as a critical design element—one of the seven Experiential Learning Variables & Indicators of ELVIS (see figure 16). In general, identity integration refers to the degree to which experiencers' identities are revealed, considered, accommodated, and/or utilized within your design of

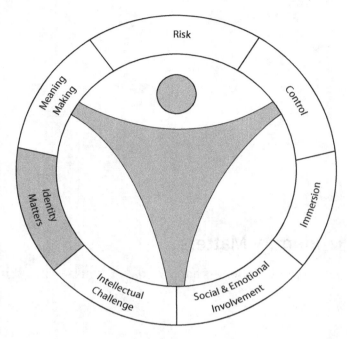

**Figure 16:** Identity Matters

an experience. It also refers to your own identity if you are designing experiences for yourself.

Recall that our operational definition of a transformative experience is one that changes an experiencer's sense of self or identity—
that is, who you believe yourself to be and/or who you aspire to
become—in some significant way. The challenge for designers here
is to incorporate experience elements that are explicitly intended to
expand participants' sense of self. As we've discussed, this begins with
a hard look at who they are going in (to the extent you can), and
then builds through expansion of who they *become* through the experience.

Clearly, then, one size does not fit all, and flexibility to tailor your
design to individuals is a key practice whenever possible. Such customized identity-based design must include methods for understanding your experiencers' identity narratives and then using that
information to better forecast and prepare for how your designed ex-

perience will land with them. To the degree you can do so, it also helps in customizing your ELVIS designs. Let's start with methods to creatively reveal experiencer identities. Together or independently, they help form an identity snapshot for both you as designer and them as experiencers. I call this "looking in the identity mirror."

## Look in the Identity Mirror

Methods for gaining an understanding of experiencer identities range from simple conversations to more intricate exercises. I like to use both. I typically use them in the pre-experience design phase so that I can apply what I learn to my design and/or invite my experiencers to participate in customizing parts of the design (participatory design strategies again). I've also used them in the post-experience phase in order to see how experiencers' sense of self may have changed over the course of the experience—the nature of the transformation, if there was one.

When we think about building an understanding of someone's identity, we are in the business of revealing their identity narratives. In most cases, the experiencers themselves are usually a little hazy on their own identity narratives until you ask them to think about themselves that way and share. It is not unusual for both of you to make important discoveries during this process of taking an identity snapshot.

My experiencers regularly tell me that exploring their "identity matters" was a critical part of the experience they were participating in. It's something they had not done before and served to deepen the impact and meaning of the overall experience for them. My observation is that by bringing identity into the mix of the other ELVIS variables and indicators and raising what would otherwise be an unconscious element to a conscious level, you invite experiencers to consider themselves and their participation in the experience in a new light. This new perspective often opens them up to multiple dimensions of an experience and causes them to invest more fully and reflect on its impacts in such a way that the possibility of personal change and transformation is increased.

When thinking about getting an identity snapshot, it is helpful to use our identity types from chapter 4 to sort the narratives you are asking them to share:

**Role identities:** Describing the various roles and functions we perform in society, such as our professional identities (our jobs), being a student, a coach, a parent, and so on.

**Social identities:** Describing how we connect to others through group affiliation, such as gender, race/ethnicity, age group, political party, religion, team membership, or even social media.

**Personal identities:** Describing elements of our sense of self that set us apart from everyone else and articulate our unique way of living a life, of being in the world, and of inhabiting our own narratives. These are the deeper stories we share only with an intimate few.

Within these types, identity narratives are revealed through self-stories, self-appraisals, reflected self-appraisals (what we think others think of us), and aspirations. When you ask people about themselves, they will automatically commingle these identity types, blending and conflating them in just the same ways as they live through them in their daily lives, as we all do. It is up to you to listen with a keen ear and hear the differences between the identity types to make the information as applicable to your ELVIS designs as possible.

So, to access experiencer identity narratives and how they generate a sense of self in a meaningful way, I use four identity activities: the Identity Interview, Narrative Timeline, Me / Not Me, and Identity in the Cards. As you read through these, try them out on yourself or with people you know. Applying them effectively is a skill that must be developed, and it starts with knowing how you will react when you are the one whose snapshot is being taken. Smile!

### Identity Activity 1: The Identity Interview

This activity is exactly what it sounds like: a guided conversation between an interviewer (you as the designer) and the interviewee (the experiencer). I try to keep these interviews to an hour, hold them in a quiet, private setting, and conduct them after I've had a chance to interact with the person and build familiarity beforehand. If I'm meeting the person for the first time, however, I make an extra effort to build rapport before the interview begins, since the topic of discussion is indeed a very personal one. The question prompts are deceptively simple, but get to the point quickly:

- How do you like to introduce yourself to strangers in professional settings, in social or recreational settings, and in personal settings? How are these introductions alike and different? Why?
- What do you hope people in those different settings think of you from your introduction?
- What are some things you like to leave out of your standard introduction? Why?
- What kinds of things will people learn about you over time as they get to know you?
- Tell me the story of how you became a [insert role, social, or personal identity here].
- What has been your most transformative experience so far? How did it change you?
- What have been your biggest triumphs and tragedies? How have they shaped you?
- What are your greatest loves, fears, and questions?
- In thinking about your future self, what aspirations do you have? How are you intending to bring those aspirations to life?
- What did I not think to ask you that might be important to know about you?

With each question, be prepared to probe more deeply. Follow where they lead. You might not have time to get through all these questions. That is fine. Choose and edit those most important to you. Be engaged and curious and remember it is about the experiencer, not about you. Epictetus said it best, "We have two ears and one mouth so we can listen twice as much as we speak."

### Identity Activity 2: Narrative Timeline

This activity borrows from the playbook of narrative therapy. The psychoanalytic practice of narrative therapy is centered on how we author our own life stories and how we can change our situations through re-storying ourselves. It was articulated by Michael White and David Epston in the 1980s, but its roots date back to famed psychologist Milton Erickson in the first half of the twentieth century, and may date back even further. A particularly useful tool in this practice is the Narrative Timeline. I present my version here. Try it out on yourself first.

Think of your life as one long *living story* with several shorter chapters or episodes. What have been the most significant plot points in your story? These can be experiences that shaped you in positive or negative ways, critical relationships, events that marked a turning point in your life, and so on up to the present. Draw a timeline on a piece of paper and plot these points in chronological order. For positive experiences, make them rise to an appropriate level of positivity relative to other plot points. For negative experiences, make them drop to an appropriate level of negativity relative to other plot points (see figure 17). Add a short annotation for each, including your age for each event.

Then, revisit these stories as contributing to the larger story of who you are today. If you can, share this living story with someone close to you. Stories live and breathe in their telling and hearing, so sitting down with your timeline and walking someone else through it in storytelling mode will make your story come alive, for both you and them.

Explore some important questions for these plot points: How were they positive or negative? How did you interpret them at the time,

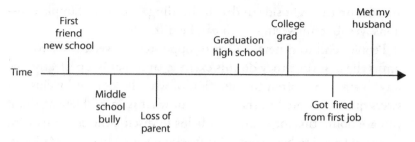

**Figure 17:** Narrative Timeline

and how do you interpret them now? What do they mean to you, and why have you carried them with you all this time? How did they affect subsequent events in your life story further downstream? How did they lead to your current life circumstances?

The Narrative Timeline activity sparks us to reflection and introspection, and it often causes us to make richer meaning out of our experiences, connect them holistically, and ultimately deepen our understanding of ourselves. In therapy situations, you might next begin the business of examining how your personal plot line is keeping you from solving your problems today and then changing your self-perceptions to healthier ones to find a new personal pathway. But for our purposes in designing transformative experiences, we examine these timelines (for ourselves or others) to see what elements of our ELVIS designs might resonate, empower, conflict, inhibit, or surprise the experiencer, and how we might tweak them to serve our experiencers better.

### Identity Activity 3: Me / Not Me

The Me / Not Me activity emerges from identity theory research and asks two simple questions about your current sense of self. Try it out on yourself first.

Draw a vertical line down a sheet of paper. Think about what best describes who you are. What is included in your definition of "me"? Write your answers on the left side under the heading "Me." Conversely, what is included in your definition of "not me"? Write your answers on the right side under the heading "Not me." Simple questions, yes, but answering them can be difficult.

People tend to generate a list of opposites between the two columns the first time they do this exercise, and that is a perfectly fine way to start. But often the question of what is "not me" yields answers quite unrelated to the answers of what is "me." Here again, if you are doing this for yourself, it helps to discuss the columns with a trusted friend to hear yourself unpacking your Me / Not Me ideas.

When doing this activity with your experiencers, the process is very much the same except that you are the facilitator. Once they generate their two lists, it is your job to probe into what they've shared:

- How is this part of who you are?
- How long has this been part of you?
- Which part of you does this describe?
- Why is this one *not* part of you? Is it intentional or just the way it is?
- Is there an experience where these lists changed at some point?

Again, your goal is to reveal their identity narratives, so ask for stories. By far the best part of this activity is to compare their Me / Not Me lists with their Narrative Timeline if you've been able to conduct both activities. Asking your experiencers to make comparisons and discover where these two activities converge and diverge and why never fails to be a rich and revealing conversation. People will tend to want the "results" of these activities to be congruent. People strive to be consistent and are happy when they are. But the hard truth is that each of us is full to the brim with inconsistencies. So when you reveal inconsistencies during these activities, be sure to reassure your experiencers that it is OK, it is normal, and it is a wonderful opportunity to explore more.

### Identity Activity 4: Identity in the Cards
Our final activity for accessing our current sense of self is the Identity in the Cards exercise. This is also one I use frequently in my research. Again, try it out on yourself first.

Grab a stack of notecards and a pen. Think about all the different identities you inhabit in your life and all the different roles you currently play in relation to others. Write each identity on a separate card. For example, I would write "father" on one card, "social scientist" on another, and so on. You can include more expansive things like "music lover," "leader," or "artist," for example. Keep writing until you have a stack of cards that pretty much sums you up at this time in your life.

Next, rank these identity cards in order of importance to you, from most important to least important. What are your most important identities right now? We know that our identities are fluid throughout our lives; therefore, both our list of identities and the priorities we assign to them will change. Use your phone to take a snapshot of your importance ranking; we will use it for comparisons later.

Next, rank your identity cards in order of how much time you spend in each identity, from most to least. This usually requires some significant rearranging from what you consider to be most important. Too often, what we deem to be the most important things in our lives are not what we spend the most time on. Again, take a quick snapshot of your ranking for later comparisons.

Last of all, consider a perfect world where everything is just the way you would want it. What would be your perfect arrangement of these cards? Would some disappear? Would some be added? Are there identities you want to have but don't? Would the order change? Are there identities you've lost, want back, or even mourn? What would be your ideal Self?

In my work, this identity card sorting activity and these rankings are often enough all by themselves to cause people to embark on some life-changing actions for themselves. In all cases, they provide us with a better understanding of ourselves now and allude to where we want to be in the future. When you do this with your experiencers, use the same sequence of steps and the same probing questions after each step. I will often snap a picture of the rankings so that I can compare them at the beginning of an experience (phase 1) with how they rank them at the end (phase 3), and then explore the changes with them. Curiously, most people I work with want to keep their cards, and many have saved them over the years.

> Listening to our identity narratives is the first step in expanding them or, in some cases, liberating ourselves from them.

Listening to our existing identity narratives is the first step in expanding them or, in some cases, liberating ourselves from them. Taken together, these simple self-appraisal exercises provide deeper notions of our starting place for designing transformative experiences for ourselves and others. Importantly, these exercises also start us on the path of internalizing control and authorship of our self-stories by giving us tools for later comparisons in order to reveal changes in our sense of self, thereby increasing our skill set for designing transformative experiences. With practice, this is something we continually get better at.

Using any or all these identity activities provides a robust way to gain a snapshot of who someone perceives themselves to be at a given moment in their lives. I also encourage you to consider adding a fifth activity: Our Intersectional Selves, which is based on the powerful activity I described in chapter 8 from the Science Museum of Minnesota. It is especially useful if you wish to highlight inclusion and diversity in your experience designs.

Now it's time to use the identity information you've collected for improving your ELVIS designs.

## How to Make Identity-Based Design Customizations

I worked with a company that, after being exposed to ELVIS, and the identity matters element in particular, radically altered their performance review practice for employees. It's a great example of how identity-based customizations can change the design of an experience for the better.

As most of us know, annual performance reviews of employees are typically dreaded perfunctory rituals where the employee fills out the same form every year to describe their work, their progress over the past year, and their goals for the next year. They then meet with their supervisor to go over it, and they both sign off, relieved the task is over. If this sounds familiar and stunningly unproductive to you, you're not alone. The idea behind performance reviews is not a bad one, but the process for conducting them is a distraction at best and a total waste of time at worst. That's why this company was shocked when I recommended they do them more frequently.

Work flowed at this company, as in most, on a quarterly rhythm: quarterly sales numbers, quarterly earnings, and quarterly stock reports and projections. Employees often lived and died by these quarterly indicators of their performance as an organization and as teams. Why not also include their performance as individuals? Well, the burdens of extra work and time were the main pushback. But as we worked on unpacking ELVIS and applying it to their culture, the idea came up that we could treat each quarter as an experience, bounded by the work and performance of those three months. Leaders could then cast themselves as designers of quarterly experiences for their direct reports, applying the tools of ELVIS to better lead and develop their teams and also invite the possibility for personal transformations of individual employees. But how to streamline shorter and more meaningful performance reviews into this model?

The first step was to change the company's annual performance review practice to an identity interview. This interview was based on the employee's professional identities and conducted once to establish a baseline and then updated quarterly to keep each individual's trajectory top of mind at the company. It also invited individuals to link their professional lives and role identities with other elements of their lives and their social and personal identities, bringing a greater sense of belonging and signaling that the company cared about them as people, not just job performers.

These identity interviews also allowed the leaders to address the other elements of ELVIS in the work plans for each employee, asking, What risks were they taking? How much control were they assuming? What social and emotional aspirations did they have? And more. Plus, they could better align the next quarter's organizational goals with the goals and aspirations of the employees. That is, they were able to design experiences on a quarterly basis that took into account the identities of their employees.

In some cases this included a greater emphasis on mentoring and sponsoring. In others it meant exploring more options for flexible work strategies. In still others, it entailed more intellectual challenges and stretch assignments. But by setting the rhythm to match the workflow and touching base with employees more frequently but more briefly using an identity-based lens, the company made sure that people felt seen for who they were. Motivation and engagement ratings went up, and attrition went down. Employees reported their work took on greater meaning and they experienced more personal growth. And no one was sad to see the annual performance review ritual put to rest.

In my own experience designs, I usually work with teams of 5 to 15 people at a time, making identity snapshotting and customization very practical. Following are some examples:

- When I learned that a participant of an international adventure of mine had never before flown on a plane or traveled outside her country, and considered herself an inexperienced and unadventurous person, I organized a special tour of the cockpit of the plane we were flying on, invited her to take leadership positions in the planned activities of the experience, and asked her to be first to share her reflections and narratives as the journey progressed.
- When I learned that a teenage boy in one of my experiences had extreme social anxiety and was deathly afraid of public speaking, considering himself to be a shy and nonconfident person, I paired him with a talented and encouraging public speaker to work together on their presentations within the experience.
- When I learned that one of my participants had hemophilia and considered himself a "handicapped" person, I devised emergency backup plans in each location we

visited in case he missed his injections or had a life-threatening injury, but insisted he participate in the experience at the same level as everyone else.

- When I learned that a corporate executive resented having to spend time on inclusion and diversity issues instead of doing "real work," but was afraid to state that for fear of being labeled "non-PC," I was able to modify a training experience to give her a stronger voice, acknowledge her views, and respectfully explore the issues she was struggling with.
- When I learned that one of my Kili climbers had journeyed all the way to Africa carrying his mother's ashes in order to spread them on the summit but could not complete the climb because of illness, we stood together at his personal summit to recognize and celebrate the quiet moment together.

When I learned . . . When I learned . . . When I learned . . . All these examples of experience design customizations are based on what I learned as the designer from pursuing identity snapshots. More than simply talking with and getting to know someone, this is the very intentional process of learning and applying the element of identity matters to experience designs. They are not always huge customizations or design changes, but they do not have to be in order to make huge differences in the hearts and minds of experiencers.

However, sometimes larger design changes are possible and/or needed. In either case, I follow a simple process for design customization.

### 1. Pre-experience Identity Sharing and Participatory Design

In addition to the four identity snapshot activities we explored above, make a point to gather your experiences in person or online at least once in the pre-experience phase so they can share some of their identity narratives with each other. This also gives you another opportunity to share the experience narrative, as you've designed it so

---

**Designer Tip**

*Pre-experience Identity Narrative Swap*

When you structure this part of the experience, be sure to explicitly describe what identity narratives are and call on your experiencers to share them (it's OK if not everyone wants to). Then start listening, making sure to validate each person's share. My favorite method for this is to sit in a circle outside and pass around a speaking stick (or other object). This mimics the age-old camp-fire ritual humans have long engaged in. In fact, on more than one occasion when I could not gather a group outside, I created a campfire setting in the office, complete with Halloween flame lights, a few logs of wood on top, and some blankets on the floor. Turn off the lights and gather the group. Voilà!

---

far, and then invite their reactions, additions, and modifications (to the extent your design can be flexible). This gets us back to participatory design (yet again), which we explored in chapter 7.

Participatory design is the first kind of identity customization to implement. By inviting your experiencers to the design table (again, to the extent your design can be flexible), you transfer a degree of control and ownership of the experience to them. They will bring their own identity factors to this invitation—their confidences, uncertainties, anxieties, preferences, and growth aspirations. They will also hear all those things from their fellow experiencers, inviting them to see the experience through the eyes of others, increasing its depth and richness, and enhancing group bonding.

## 2. ELVIS by Element

By the time the pre-experience phase begins, I, as the designer, have already mapped out the experience element by element using ELVIS for the whole group. At this point, after I've collected identity snapshots from my experiencers, I revisit each ELVIS element to consider it through the lens of each experiencer's identity, or what I've come to learn about them so far. This means applying many of the same questions you've been seeing at the end of each chapter here in part 2 of the book, but applying them to each person, based on what I have learned about them.

Instead of asking, "To what extent can experiencers make risk decisions within the experience?," I would ask, "To what extent might *Jim* make risk decisions within the experience?"

Instead of asking, "How would you describe experiencers' 'personal ownership' of the experience in terms of their ability to contribute to its design and/or implementation?," I would ask, "How would you describe *Shana's* likely 'personal ownership' of the experience in terms of her ability to contribute to its design and/or implementation?"

Instead of asking, "How would you describe the way intellectual challenges are encountered by experiencers in your design?," I would ask, "How would you describe the way intellectual challenges might be encountered by *Simone* in your design?"

And so on. For the ELVIS element of risk in particular, I use the risk profiles I've created for my experiencers (see chapter 6) to add more detail to how I might customize risk invitations for different people.

By taking my basic design and the answers to these ELVIS design questions, and then considering it through the identity lenses of each experiencer, I become better able to anticipate their possible individual reactions to my design. And even if I'm not always right (and I'm right only about half the time), the attention to this important perspective throughout the experience makes it far less likely I will miss opportunities to alter the design in customized ways for each experiencer, such as arranging a cockpit tour or partnering a person with low agency for public speaking with a person who has high agency.

### Designer Tip

#### *ELVIS by Element for Individuals*

You can also do this using participatory design. Invite your experiencers to directly answer the questions listed above for themselves. Most times, this requires people to imagine how they will feel and react during the experience to come, but no one really knows for sure. However, projecting in this way reveals aspirations and anxieties and serves to frame and prime the forthcoming experience and the narrative they will generate from it.

### 3. ELVIS as Evaluation

Finally, one of the most powerful customization tools brings the designer out of the world of their own speculation (which is prone to biases and cognitive distortions of all kinds) and asks experiencers themselves to directly respond to the ELVIS design questions. This is best done during the experience phase of the design when they have something to provide feedback on, and while there are still opportunities to modify the design because it is not over yet. I will present my experiencers with the ELVIS toolkit design questions just as I used them in developing my design, and ask them to respond in reference to a particular component of the experience or even the entire experience up to that point. Visit the companion site for this book for a complete set of the ELVIS Design Questions and Matrix in one easy-to-use package: DesigningTransformativeExperiences.com.

Not only can I then compare their answers with what I had designed and intended for different elements of the experience, but I can also examine the differences between individual experiencer's responses and what I learned from their identity snapshots to gain an excellent idea of how the experience is going for them. I can then consider if they need a jolt here or there, if they need

---

**Designer Tip**

***ELVIS as Evaluation Post-experience***

If you simply don't have the time and energy to do this while your designed experience is unfolding, it is well worthwhile to do it in the post-experience phase. Used then, this tool can become the structure for the individual meaning making that occurs most intensely after the main experience is over. You can focus on some or all the ELVIS 7, depending on the details of your design and your group. By analyzing the gaps between what you intended and what your team experienced and making this part of your normal leadership reflective practice, you'll get better and better at aligning your ELVIS designs with your experiencers' identity growth.

more encouragement, more risk, more social support, and so on. In short, I ask myself what design customizations can I make and for whom.

This is in situ Experience Design Leadership using the ELVIS lens for maximum impact. And, yes, all this takes time and structure when you might already be up to your gills in other leadership tasks. But this is what makes ELVIS different from all other leadership approaches in placing experiencers at the center.

## When Customizations Aren't Possible

Despite your best aspirations and expertise in experience design, sometimes you are not able to customize designs for the identities of your cohorts. Sometimes the designs are rigid in terms of content, timing, or sequence. Sometimes you do not have the time or luxury of gathering much information about experiencer identities, if at all. Sometimes you have to use blanket assumptions about who your audience may be and design to the median.

In these cases, I make a point to use parallel design strategies. This means providing multiple options for different experiencers to select from in terms of what they engage in or how. In the conference I hosted on transformative experiences that I discussed above, for example, I had over 400 attendees. Identity snapshots and experience customization were just not practical. So, I made it a point to include highly active and athletic experiences (such as rock climbing or scuba diving) as well as highly cerebral and more sedentary experiences (such as mobile apps design, robotics, and cell phone photography). To the extent I could, then, I gave the power of choice and a degree of control over to my experiencers.

This approach also gave them control to take risks beyond what I would've designed for them. For example, I had a paraplegic woman in a wheelchair who opted for GoPro paragliding. Other great examples include home exercise programs such as Tonal (my personal favorite) and Peloton. These programs brilliantly meet the problem of not knowing individual users' identities by employing parallel design strategies to create challenging experiences with multiple levels of participant choice and control, as well as multiple opportunities for personal interaction with coaches and other users.

Whether you have a lot of structure and capability for identity-based design customization or almost none, it is best to avoid one-size-fits-all or one-size-fits-most approaches whenever and wherever you can. Remember, the experience resides within your experiencers. Transformative experiences always come from within. And there is where we must center our ELVIS designs in whatever ways we can through choice, options, and experiencer control.

## Emergence in Identity Matters

In the more dramatic experiences I used to lead (trips to exotic places to do daring things), I started to notice another experience element that I had not consciously designed for. My experiencers started to speak of it in their reflections and in their narrative translations of a given experience. It happened so often that I ultimately began to intentionally design for it whenever I could. It is the "cathartic experience."

This is the idea that the whole experience builds toward or sometimes hinges on a lofty element, or a big scary goal. As I described in previous chapters, for my Tanzania experience designs it was climbing Mount Kilimanjaro at nearly 20,000 feet. For Zero-G it was floating weightless inside a careening 727. For the Hawaii journey it was traversing Devastation Trail or shark diving. Other elements or activities within the design were important, but they were often seen as the preamble to the "main event."

At least this is the way experiencers would forecast and anticipate their challenges beforehand. However, as I described earlier, oftentimes their view of what was cathartic would change during the post-experience design phase where meaning making would take place. For example, as I described in chapter 3, my Africa experiencers would often cite Kili as the big scary goal going in and their most significant for a while post-journey, but would later describe their interactions with the everyday people of Tanzania, working in schools and AIDS orphanages as the most impactful elements.

I came to notice a real value to the construction of a catharsis challenge. It motivated experiencers to prepare for and invest in the experience. It was a source of internal permission that gave them control and ownership, and it gave them bragging rights with their friends and colleagues. It was more powerfully linked to their identity growth.

But a catharsis need not be an act of deathless daring. The word "catharsis" refers to a purging or discharge of pent-up emotion, tension, and expectation. The catharsis challenge is the peak of the experience, when vulnerability and risk are at their highest. The catharsis challenge leads to the actual catharsis—the release that follows. In my ELVIS designs nowadays, I think of catharsis challenges as what an experiencer considers the area of highest risk and lowest agency for them in my design, depending on their identity going in. My operational design definition for a catharsis challenge has become the following:

*An experience element that powerfully challenges an experiencer's initial identity narrative, initiating a change process that includes letting go of their prior sense-of-self in some way, and inviting new self-perceptions.*

What emerges when we design for experiences that are customized to challenge experiencer identity narratives is a result of their meaning making (the subject of the next chapter) before, during, and most importantly after an experience.

## ELVIS Design Questions: Identity Matters
1. **To what extent are experiencers' identities considered or integrated into the experience design?**
    1. The experience design is one-size-fits-all with no accommodation of individual experiencer identities.

2. The experience design is mostly one-size-fits-all but includes limited efforts to establish personal relevancy and attends to experiencer preferences, abilities, motivations, or expectations.

3. The experience design is equally balanced between pre-established plans and efforts to establish personal relevancy and attends to participant preferences, abilities, motivations, or expectations.

4. The experience design is mostly based on the identities of experiencers and seeks to establish personal relevancy and attend to participant preferences, abilities, motivations, or expectations but includes some limited one-size-fits-all elements.

5. The experience is designed based on the identities of the experiencers as the central organizing framework.

2. **To what extent are changes in or expansions of experiencers' identity narratives considered for assessment of impact or definitions of success?**

1. Experiencer identity narratives are not considered for design assessments or goals for success.

2. Changes to experiencer identity narratives are a minor component of the design assessments or goals for success.

3. Changes to experiencer identity narratives are equally considered for design assessments or goals for success along with other program goals.

4. Changes to experiencer identity narratives are the dominant element for design assessments or definitions for success along with other program goals or definitions of success.

5. Design assessment and definitions for success are based on changes to experiencer identity narratives.

3. **How would you describe the incorporation of personal catharsis challenges into the experience design?**

1. There are no challenges (personally tailored or otherwise) designed into the experience.

2. Some limited challenges are designed into the experience but are not personally tailored to the identities of participants.
3. Challenges are an important part of the experience design and include some flexible elements that can be tailored to the identities of experiencers.
4. Challenges that are personally tailored to the identities of experiencers are an important part of the design but are not intended to be cathartic.
5. Cathartic challenges that are personally tailored to the identities of experiencers are central to the experience design.

Total for all questions: _____
ELVIS Zone (average score): _____

## 12 ■ Meaning Making

Forging Personal Relevance and Designing
to Support That Process

*Whoever controls information, whoever controls meaning, acquires power.*

—Laura Esquivel,
*Malinche*

Meaning making is the last of the ELVIS 7 (see figure 18). As all of our experiences are ultimately transformed into narratives, the process of meaning making occurs through the wonderfully rich and multifaceted generation of personal narratives. Recall that for experiences to be transformative, the experience narratives must in some way inform, influence, or modify our identity narratives. How can designers facilitate this meaning-making process with their experiencers? To explore this, let's start with a story within a story.

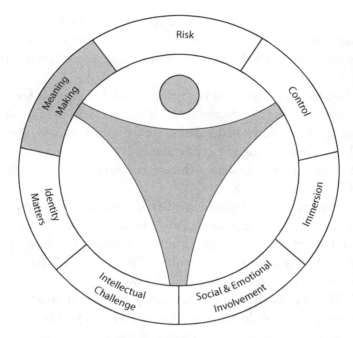

**Figure 18:** Meaning Making

## A Fall into Parenthood: What I Learned from 14 Stairs, a Dog Bite, and Primal Instinct

In graduate school, I was once asked to narrate an experience that somehow changed me. As a new father at the time, I decided to share a unique experience about becoming a first-time parent, one of the most transformative experiences that can happen to a person. As I relived the experience in my memory, I began to sequence it into narrative form, adding internal perspectives to external events, describing emotions and conflicts along with self-discoveries and self-changes. I was engaging in a process of meaning making that changed how I saw myself as a dad. It's a powerful example of delayed identity transformation, as you will see. Many times, the most pivotal thresholds that we cross are only recognizable as

> Many times, the most pivotal thresholds that we cross are only recognizable as such in the rearview mirror.

such in the rearview mirror or through the eyes of close family and friends who notice transformation within us before we can see it in ourselves. My example went something like the following paragraphs.

I had resigned myself to not being a dad. I was just a few years into my marriage. My then-wife (such a better term than "ex-wife," in my opinion) and I had decided to try for kids, a decision that ushered in an astonishing string of consecutive miscarriages (six "officially," another nine probably, though the parade of seven different doctors couldn't be sure).

I remember our first pregnancy. My wife presented the pregnancy test evidence. "Two pink lines. Two," she said. Her smile was ear to ear and uncontrollable. "I don't know. . . . That second line is pretty faint . . . barely there at all," I doubted. "But it's there," she asserted. "If it's there at all, it's a done deal." We were so naive.

Within weeks, the ultrasounds that previously showed a cluster of growing cells would show nothing. We had no problems whatsoever getting pregnant. It was staying pregnant that eluded us. We simply could not come to term. I say "we," and wonder why. My wife bore the brunt—the emotional cacophony, the hormonal banshee possessing her, the pain and the blood. I, on the other hand, was a useless spectator to the drama unfolding before me, an increasingly distant audience to my own life.

The scariest part came in year four. My wife walked out of the bathroom late one night and announced she'd miscarried again. I'd lost count of what number it was by then. I was in bed reading a book while our dog Indy slept nearby. I simply nodded, rolled over, and kept reading. Inside I was terrified. I was devastated at the first miscarriage. Was it now routine? I had become the transparent ghost of bystandery, disguised as a human being. But, at least I was terrified. That was something.

The eighth doctor was different. She asked questions for the better part of an hour and listened to our stories—not only the biological facts but all the rest of it too: How we avoided discussing kids with anyone these days. How I secretly resented and wanted to throttle any parent who complained about or showed any level of impatience with their children. How we, upon revealing the miscarriages to friends, were suddenly inundated with stories from other couples who had their own hidden miscarriage tales, apparently pulled out and dusted off in commiseration for reluctant new members of this sadly large secret club.

"Let's draw some blood, do some tests," she said. "I have a hunch." Days later, she confirmed a maternal genetic blood disorder that caused blood thickening, effectively cutting off microcirculation in the placenta. We finally had an answer. And we had a treatment: blood thinners. Our aged hearts were suddenly young again. Six months later, my wife was pregnant again. She was glowing, but I kept waiting for the other shoe to drop. I waited until halfway through the second trimester—the day I felt my child kick for the first time—before I permitted myself to get excited.

The night before the birth was ethereal. As she drifted off to sleep, I paced. Isn't that what expectant fathers do? I scrutinized the monitors all night. I had learned what each number, icon, sound, and animated line meant. I especially watched the one depicting the two heartbeats, keenly aware that my whole life was somehow strangely concentrated in the two people contained in one body on the bed just over there.

Kai emerged early the next morning, tiny and perfect. When they placed him in my arms, he looked at me with his baby eyes sparkling and new. I was to be struck through the heart, bonded instantly, forever and always . . . was I not? But I was not. I was moved, profoundly, but I was waiting for what all the parenting books had foretold: Everything will change forever when you hold your child for the first time. You will know your life is forfeit for this new creature now in your care. Well, I was holding him, waiting for it . . . staring . . . and wondering. Why wasn't I feeling that ineffable bond?

I had excuses to relieve me. I was overstimulated. I was tired, not having slept all night. I was worried about my wife . . . anything, anything at all, please, but what I feared: that after all this time I still could not feel. I was waiting for the one thing that would prove I had returned from my emotional exile. Truly, what was wrong with me?

As the months passed, I managed to put aside my private humanity crisis and concentrated instead on the sleepless duties new parents know. It was a happy burden, no matter the hour, no matter the need or request. I delighted in the sound of Kai's cry, a new music filling the house. But in my private moments, still I waited.

On a sunny April morning, a newly standing Kai shakily stood at the top of 14 stairs leading down to the kitchen. I was getting ready for the day a dozen paces away. The doorbell rang. Indy, our 50-pound dog, leapt to his feet barking. In his obsessed haste to get downstairs and confront the visitor at the door, Indy careened directly into Kai like a battering ram, knocking him down the flight of stairs. I rushed out of the bedroom, inches out of reach. In the slow motion of traumatic events, Kai tumbled log-like down each step with Indy barking and leaping immediately behind him all the way down as I helplessly stumbled after them both. As Kai reached the bottom with a horrifying thud, I was certain Indy would land right on top of him with his sharp claws and crazed tunnel vision to get to the door. To my relief, Indy expertly jumped over Kai. I swept in to take Kai up in my arms.

There was a breathless pause, then suddenly it came, a massive emotional release from us all—the fearful scream from Kai (thankfully he was OK), the panic-stricken look on my wife's face, and then my own erupting rage at Indy for nearly killing my son. I handed Kai to my wife. Without thinking, in a blind primal frenzy I'd never known before, I seized Indy, grabbing handfuls of fur and skin at his neck and rump. I savagely lifted him with a canine-like growl to bodily toss him into the kitchen. As I hefted him, he reflexively turned and sank his sharp teeth deep into my hand, with a bloody rip.

Indy ran off to another room. I slowly became dizzy and nauseous. I couldn't tell if it was from the bite or the events of the last 15 seconds. My hand was bleeding freely, throbbing and swelling. There was blood all over the floor. I suddenly discovered I was soaked in sweat, head to toe. Indy's tooth had penetrated deep into the middle joint capsule of my index finger. The emergency room doctors had to deeply irrigate and clean it every four hours for days, and were infusing me with the most powerful antibiotics they had to fight the infection and save my finger. On day three, a plastic surgeon came in to discuss amputation.

I sat there amid the evidence of my stupidity—my bandaged hand, an IV in my arm, pain pills on the table. How could I have been so reckless? To take the gate off the stairs with Kai still up there, to not put Indy outside as usual in the mornings, and then to grab him in anger even after the danger had passed . . . I deserved to get bitten. But there was something else.

A deep peace swept over me. I had acted primally, instinctively, immediately, without thought. My rage at Indy was irrational, stupid even, but perfectly clear and powerfully simple. Somehow, over the past several months without my knowing, it happened. I was forever bonded to Kai. The universe had forgiven my original emotional sin against the privilege of fatherhood, through the redemptive bite of a dog, and awakened me to a new life. In the end, Kai was OK. Indy and I made up, I got to keep my finger, and I was no longer waiting. I had become Kai's dad.

I share this story as another example of a transformative experience, of course, but also as an example of meaning making. In constructing the narrative for a class assignment, I forged a new understanding of those events from a different perspective—the narrator. In so doing, I became aware of the importance of the experience to my identity as a dad. I made meaning that I would not have otherwise done.

How can designers of transformative experiences use this same psychology to equip experiencers with this opportunity as well?

### Embedded Meaning Making: A Critical Path for Transformation
Strategies and tools for meaning making are best applied throughout an experience as embedded components. While depth of meaning can be found with bake time and in retrospection (such as my experience becoming Kai's dad), those processes are greatly aided

by embedding narrative tools within an experience. But too often, leaders, teachers, parents, or coaches reserve all reflection and meaning making for the very end of an experience, if they do it at all. However, when we integrate narrative-building elements into our ELVIS designs, we give our experiencers a wonderful gift, that of the conscious participant-narrator.

> When we integrate narrative-building elements into our ELVIS designs, we give our experiencers a wonderful gift, that of the conscious participant-narrator.

Some people claim that embedded reflection interrupts an experience. I agree, if it is done poorly. When we assign our experiencers the role of participant-narrator, we position them as real-time story builders. This is different from storytellers, whose job begins only when the events of an experience end. By embedding meaning making throughout our ELVIS designs, we invite experiencers to more deeply consider and reflect on the experience *as it happens.*

This highly conscious attention to what is presently occurring serves to enrich the experience with that "in the moment" feeling and captures the small details that are often lost otherwise. If you've ever kept a journal but didn't have time to write in it every day, you know how hard it is days or weeks later to recall all the juicy little tidbits, conversations, or even the challenges, aspirations, and uncertainties you've experienced. Authentic in situ questions like "What is going to happen?" "How will I do?" and "What is happening and how am I responding?" can only be asked while the experience is unfolding. It is at that time that curiosity and wonder are excited, and risk and uncertainty are identified and explored. Plus, experiencer thinking and feeling are made visible (a huge asset for designers).

If we always wait to do this kind of narration and reflection until after the events have passed, and *only* do it then, we run the risk of foisting a narrative structure onto our experiences that is less genuine and more likely to be based on preexisting templates and clichés, such as heroically achieving the goal, struggling to win the game, or failing miserably to get the job.

The world is too well worn with the deep ruts of uninspiring narratives through which it pressures us to live our lives and forge our identities. Your life, your story, your lens, and your way of being in the world are unique, as are those of your experiencers. Author your own narrative, and empower others to author theirs.

The world is too well worn with the deep ruts of uninspiring narratives through which it pressures us to live our lives and forge our identities.

**Embedded Meaning-Making Strategies and Tools**
For experience designers, the methods for embedded meaning making must include incorporating multiple structured ways for people to become self-aware authors of their personal experiences. This can include both multiple methods (discussions, journaling, video creation, etc.) and multiple times for meaning making during an experience. For overall strategy, we break it down by experience design phase with basic plans and prompts for any generic experience. You no doubt will need to adapt these for your specific ELVIS designs as needed, scaling their scope and depth back for shorter and smaller experiences, while diving deeper for more involved experiences.

*Pre-experience Design Phase: The Ground under Your Feet*
Every journey begins exactly where you are. Experiencers' meaning making starts with the identity narratives they bring with them. The tools we discussed in chapter 11, "Identity Matters," can be incredibly useful for experiencers to ground themselves in the pre-experience design phase. Additional instructions and prompts I use for experiencer journaling or videos or discussions in this grounding are answers to basic questions:

The following prompts are designed to establish your starting place for this experience—to provide a snapshot of the ground from which you will proceed:

- Who am I today, about to embark on this experience?
- What events have brought me here?

- What current and past experiences am I bringing with me that may be relevant?
- What aspirations am I hoping to fulfill and how will I know when I have?
- What risks and concerns do I have?

The answers to these questions in phase 1 "set the table" for the events to come. By starting our experiencers out in this narrative space, we tie all that will follow directly to their existing identity narratives. As I always tell my groups, "I do not want a story about the events and places and tasks of the experience; I want the story only YOU can tell—the story of YOU engaged in this experience." In the course of building that kind of story, personal meaning is made.

*Experience Design Phase: Real-Time Narration*

In the experience design phase, two things are going on for meaning making:

1. Events are occurring and experiencers are capturing those events through whatever narrative tools you've designed for (more on this below).
2. Experiencers are having anticipations and reactions to those events.

Here are the instructions and prompts I use with experiencers for this phase:

The following prompts are designed to help structure your reflections in story form. Use some or all of them on any given day to record your experience:

- Preparation and Anticipation: What preparations are you making today? What are your hopes, expectations, and concerns?
- Events: What happened today? Include the setting, context, people involved, events, actions, outcomes. How did you think and feel about these?

- Risks: What risks did you take today? What challenges did you face? What were the outcomes? How did you think and feel about these?
- Surprises: What unexpected events or outcomes occurred? How did you think and feel about these?
- Cohort: How did the group do today? What was your level of social engagement? How did you think and feel it?
- Reflections: How did the day affect you personally? What did you learn? What questions emerged? What feelings, thoughts, or meanings did you experience?
- Big Picture: How do you link today's experiences to: The larger experience? The bigger picture of your professional and personal trajectory? Your own sense-of-self?

I have found that the frequency of attending to these questions is key. It may not always be practical to do it daily, but regularly is important. Also, structuring special times, places, and orchestrated events for them to record and share their thoughts is critical.

Centerpiece experiences of your design, whether approaching big scary goals, tackling difficult tasks, facing down a big deadline, or taking on any other large risk invitations, are crucial points for meaning making. Often they are the catharsis challenges. I recommend honoring these high risk invitations and risk decisions on the part of your experiencers by organizing group reflections before and/or immediately after they occur. Remember, meaning making through narrative is not a separate part of the experience; it is a designed part of it.

> Meaning making through narrative is not a separate part of the experience, it is a designed part of it.

### Post-experience Design Phase

The post-experience design phase is the coalescence phase of the experience. The unknowns are now known. The risk decisions have all been made. The outcomes are now history. And the ripple effects have begun. The prompts I use for this phase serve as identity-based bookends to the ones we began with:

> The following prompts are designed to establish your ending place for this experience—to provide a snapshot of the ground of being you have arrived at as a result:
>
> - Who am I now as this experience ends? How have I changed?
> - How were my aspirations for participating in this experience fulfilled, or not?
> - What did I learn? What did I discover about myself?
> - How did past experiences serve me or work against me?
> - How did my relationships to others contribute during the experience?
> - What ripple effects are happening in my life because of this experience?"

Here, people often struggle to synthesize all they have captured, recorded, and collected from the narrative tools embedded within each phase of the design. I make it very simple for them by outlining a three-act structure for their story (no matter the format: oral, written, audio, video) that flows with the 3 × 3 Nested Design Strategy from chapter 5. I will often liken it to rafting a stretch of a river.

**Act 1: Putting In (Pre-experience Phase).** Establish the initial conditions: Who is telling this story? What is the nature of the experience about to be had? Why are you here, and what do you hope, fear, and wonder for the events to come? The answers to the prompts for the pre-experience phase go here.

**Act 2: Shooting the Rapids (Experience Phase).** Chronicle the events and your reactions to them: the rises and falls, the bumps and spills, the anxieties and uncertainties, the surprises and outcomes. These are your plot points around which your story turns. The answers to the prompts for the experience phase go here.

**Act 3: Exiting (Post-experience Phase).** This is the catharsis—what it all means to you. What did you learn? What did you discover about yourself? How did you change? What changes are rippling into and through your life? The answers to the prompts for the post-experience phase go here.

But there is more to act 3. Immediately after an experience that holds transformative potential, there is often an initial euphoria for experiencers. There is a first-draft narrative that results from this euphoria. But as I've mentioned several times, meanings and narratives change with bake time. One way I've dealt with this is to extend the creation of act 3 by a few weeks in order to allow time and perspective to work their magic on experiencer perceptions of what an experience means to them.

Finally, there is a shadow act: act 4, the sharing of experiencer stories with each other and other audiences. Through the storytelling process, the narrative often takes on a new life borne from the reactions of others and the interactions with the narrator. This is especially true for transformative experiences when they are shared. They always have additional impacts, sometimes positive and sometimes negative, on those closest to the transformed experiencer. But in either case, these can only be revealed when the experiencer shares their narrative (act 4). As designers we cannot design for this, but we can be aware of it and alert our experiencers to the fact that their loved ones may have varied reactions to their narrative of transformation.

> Transformative experiences always have additional impacts on those closest to the transformed experiencer.

*Embedded Narrative Tools*

The embedded meaning-making design strategies presented above can apply to any narrative tools you might choose to use. The one thing they should have in common, however, is that they are used for autobiographical storytelling. Here I present the ones I've used the most, and almost always used in various combinations with each other.

**Journaling:** A mainstay of all my experience designs, journaling is old-school paper-and-ink writing. I always provide prompts, variations of what I described above, and I also give permission to be creative: "Feel free to include anything and everything that helps you creatively capture your experience . . . sketches, painting, pictures, clippings, rubbings, taped-in samples, guest entries. Let it be messy. Experience is a messy business!" It is perhaps unsurprising that experiencer journals (even among nonjournaling kinds of people) end up becoming some of their most prized possessions when transformations occur, evoking times and places and faces that will never come again.

**Blogging, posting, and social media tools:** Cell phone usage has grown exponentially as a valuable tool for recording and sharing our lived experiences. This includes blogging, posting photos and videos, engaging in real-time and recorded social media, and much more. I have come to encourage their use and unparalleled capabilities for creative narrative authorship. I now routinely use them to support videos and audio capturing the moment, posting and sharing with friends, family, and audiences beyond the design.

**Podcasting:** In some of my experience designs I've given experiencers the option of creating podcasts about their experiences, individually or in pairs. This includes regular audio journaling, recording conversations, conducting interviews, and basically putting together an extended "radio show" (for those of you more familiar with the radio format) about their experiences using the same prompts as any other medium.

**Discovery groups:** The discovery groups I convene are very open-ended. One of my favorite techniques to use with these groups is the Hi-Lo activity. In this activity, each person simply shares their highest and lowest experiences since the last discovery group. This launches a highly interactive discussion where participants question one another, support one another, explore their similarities and differences, and ultimately co-narrate their experiences by seeing them through the eyes of the larger cohort in addition to their own. My role in these discussions is quite minimal. I validate. I thank. I sometimes supply probing questions and keep the discussion moving along. At first, groups are often a little tight-lipped and shy. But over time, "discovery grouping" is a rewarding skill that they develop and appreciate.

**Story circles:** These are different from discovery groups. Instead of conversations, story circles are much more akin to open-mic night at the local pub. Each person gets 5 to 10 minutes in the spotlight to tell a story about their experience. The duty of the rest of the cohort is simply to listen, nothing more. Conversations often break out later, after the story circle has closed, but the storytellers go in with the often reassuring knowledge that they will not have to answer questions or explain themselves—just share their stories. It also encourages them to create well-formed narratives within the experience design phase, an excellent building block toward their ultimate narrative translation of the whole experience.

**Autobiographical videos:** This is my favorite and (in my opinion) the most powerful tool for embedded narrative creation. And with cell phones and tablets now equivalent to all-in-one video production houses in a small device, it is easier than ever. The approach here is simple. I explain to my experiencers that they will be making a movie about themselves to share with others. But it is about themselves having this experience. Sometimes they do this individually or in pairs or on teams. In all cases, I tell them that they are to be the stars of their movies. Their films should chronicle their outward and inward journey through the experience, capturing their private thoughts as well as their group interactions. It can include the rich tools at their disposal: music, narration, on-screen text, self-interviews,

> **Designer Tip**
>
> *Use Embedded Narrative Tools in Concert*
>
> Each of these tools is powerful on its own, but when used in combination with others, their effect is amplified. Just as people learn in different ways, they also narrate in different ways. By designing for multiple modes of story creation and storytelling, you can reach more of your experiencers, and they can tap into more levels of their experience as they create more varied kinds of stories.

interviews with others, and more. I have them do video capture during the experience combined with their journaling. And in the post-experience design phase I have them watch all their clips, forge a narrative outline with storyboards, and edit together their creative masterpiece. Then, I organize a film festival some months after the experience in which they share their videos with the cohort. The reunion is usually a most enlightening and cathartic conclusion to an experience.

## Emergence in Meaning Making

Perhaps the most surprising and undesigned emergent outcome for embedded meaning making is that experiencers often wind up using these tools in their own lives and leadership later on. I've had many people contact me years later after participating in an experience I designed and describe how they later adopted the tools for narrative construction and meaning making in their work, with their students, with their families, and in their own lives.

Diving deeply into the art of meaning making through narrative construction is strangely addicting. It causes us to take on a different perspective for our lives and ourselves. I first got a glimpse of this when I used autobiographical video production on the Zero-G experience I described in chapter 7. Experiencers came to thank me months later for tasking them with personal video production, describing how it tremendously enhanced their experiences. I have since come to include it in many of my research projects, generating multiple ways to extract social science data from such videos for analysis and interpretation.

Perhaps the most powerful is the director's commentary. This is where I ask experiencers to produce two versions of their videos: one for screening with others and another that contains a new audio track: their running commentary as the video's director. This self-interview describes the video creation choices they made, why they chose this music or that, what they were trying to convey with this scene, and so on. The insights for me as a social scientist have been tremendous. The insights for them as experiencers have amplified their meaning-making skills and transferred to their lives beyond the design of the experiences we shared.

**ELVIS Design Questions: Meaning Making**
1. **How would you describe the incorporation of reflective practice (referring to any strategies that promote experiencer reflection) within the experience?**
   1. Reflective practice is not part of the experience design in any way.
   2. Reflective practice is not explicitly part of the design but may occur by accident or if experiencers choose to do so privately.
   3. Reflective practice is a part of the experience design but often occurs only at or near the end of the experience. It is semistructured or unstructured.
   4. Reflective practice is an important part of the experience design and occurs both during and after the experience in a structured way.
   5. Reflective practice is central to the design. Experiencers are explicitly encouraged and supported to engage in personal reflection before the experience, during the experience, and after the experience.
2. **To what extent are experiencers encouraged to construct personal narratives about the experience?**

1. Personal narrative construction is not encouraged in the experience design at any point.
2. Personal narrative construction is acceptable but not explicitly encouraged in the experience design.
3. Personal narrative construction is encouraged along with other forms of reflection but is not explicitly designed into the experience.
4. Personal narrative construction is encouraged along with other forms of reflection and is explicitly designed into the experience.
5. Personal narrative construction is the primary form of reflection explicitly encouraged in the experience design, and there are multiple structured opportunities for it throughout the design (not just at the beginning and/or end).

3. **To what extent are the following supports or structures used to facilitate experiencer meaning making?**

| Embedded reflections (think books, concept maps, feedback, etc.) | 1 not used | 2 unstructured | 3 post-only | 4 pre-post | 5 pre, during, post |
|---|---|---|---|---|---|
| **Journaling** | 1 | 2 | 3 | 4 | 5 |
| **Discovery groups** (or peer group sharing) | 1 | 2 | 3 | 4 | 5 |
| **Social media** | 1 | 2 | 3 | 4 | 5 |
| **Autobiographical story making / storytelling** | 1 | 2 | 3 | 4 | 5 |
| **Other** | 1 | 2 | 3 | 4 | 5 |

4. **How would you describe the opportunities for experiencers to share and discuss their personal reflections?**
   1. There are no opportunities for experiencers to share and discuss their personal reflections.

2. Opportunities for experiencers to share and discuss their personal reflections are neither intended nor unintended. If it occurs, it is accidental.

3. There is at least one opportunity for experiencers to share and discuss their personal reflections, and it is explicitly designed into the experience.

4. There are multiple opportunities for experiencers to share and discuss their personal reflections, and they are explicitly designed into the experience.

5. There are multiple opportunities for experiencers to share and discuss their personal reflections before, during, and after the experience. These opportunities are highly structured and explicitly designed into the experience.

5. **To what extent are experiencers' meaning-making reflections considered for assessment of impact or definitions of success?**

1. Experiencer reflections are not considered for design assessments or goals for success.

2. Experiencer reflections are a minor component of the design assessments or goals for success.

3. Experiencer reflections are equally considered for design assessments along with other outcomes.

4. Experiencer reflections are the dominant element for design assessments or definitions for success along with other program goals or definitions of success.

5. Design assessment and definitions for success are based on experiencer reflections.

Total for all questions: _____
ELVIS Zone (average score): _____

# 13 ■ The Holistic ELVIS

*The shot will only go smoothly when it takes the archer himself by surprise.*

—Eugen Herrigel,
*Zen in the Art of Archery*

As I stated when we embarked on this journey, designing transformative experiences requires us to engage in events that fundamentally challenge us from within, often dramatically removing our normal perspectives on life in order to encounter ourselves and the world in a new way. If you've made it this far in the book, you now have a deep and nuanced understanding of what ELVIS Experience Design Leadership entails and a robust set of Experiential Learning Variables and Indicators (ELVIS) tools to use in your own experience designs.

As a leadership approach, ELVIS resonates with deep-seated, ancient, and powerful undercurrents in the human experience. The business of intentionally designing transformative experiences is about bringing this psychological and spiritual inheritance from a mostly unconscious level to a conscious one so that we can harness it to empower self-determined identity growth. Have you heard the old psychologist's joke: how many psychologists does it take to change a lightbulb? Just one, but the lightbulb has to really want to change. So, too, when it comes to designing transformative experiences for ourselves or others; we must be willing to answer this call to experiential adventure. We must be willing to look hard in the mirror to know who it is that is answering the call, and we must be willing to change.

Despite having done it for over 50 years, legendary American singer-songwriter Neil Diamond described performing on stage as a transformative experience that felt new every time. His explanation is an identity self-appraisal that nicely synthesizes the design elements we've been examining. To begin with, his on-stage persona was very different from his everyday identity. "I'm basically a very quiet person," he explained to NPR radio host Scott Simon. "You wouldn't pick me out in a crowd." But before a show, "the questions are there, the doubts of course—until you get up on stage and you face the thousands of people that have come. At that point you become an entirely different person. I'm excited! I'm out of myself. I'm out of my mind and my body, into another Neil. And he's a Neil that's been living in me for years and years and years, but he only comes out when I get on stage. I like to bring him out" (NPR Weekend Edition Saturday. Aired December 17, 2016).

Now, I am aware that in a chapter titled "The Holistic ELVIS" I am here highlighting the illustrious Neil Diamond. It's an irony I hope and believe both Neil Diamond and Elvis Presley would appreciate.

Diamond's account of what it was like for one of the world's most successful and seasoned singers to perform defines an experience that alters his sense of self; that includes risk and discomfort; that is social, emotional, and intellectual in nature; with feelings of being fully immersed—ironically, "out of his mind and body." And it happens over and over. Further, his story relating the experience of performing is a relationship narrative about him and another Neil entirely and the audience, separate from his normal identity. But most interestingly, as I've observed when people describe their transformative experiences, Diamond's self-appraisal places the origin and control of this experience external to himself. "It just happens," he says. "I didn't make it happen. . . . It's something that occurs *to* me, and not something that I *make* occur." In this way he echoes what Jane Goodall described in chapter 3 as her alter ego, the celebrity "Jane Goodall creature," as something that is "not her fault."

Transformative experiences ultimately come from within, but when they predominantly emerge from our unconscious and/or involve strong external circumstances, they can convincingly seem as though they are external to us. And as we discussed earlier, conscious versus unconscious is not necessarily a binary condition but rather more often a continuum. How aware are we of the difference between what happens *to* us and what we *make* happen? Where is the line between them? And how can we push that line closer to the "making things happen" end of the spectrum? This is a challenge we face in designing transformative experiences: how to raise the level of conscious awareness for transformative experiences so that experiencers (ourselves included) can generate them intentionally. And this is where the power of using ELVIS holistically really shines.

When you, as a leader, design experiences that intentionally and consciously attend to the ELVIS 7, you invite your experiencers to do so as well as they live through it. And the more of the ELVIS 7 you attend to, the better. More often than not, this uncovers experiential treasures to you both that would've been inaccessible otherwise. As you have likely noticed throughout part 2 of this book, the ELVIS 7 are not hermetically sealed off from each other. They overlap with and flow into one another. To attempt to deal with them independently is to miss out on the holistic power of ELVIS, which is much greater than the sum of its parts.

Business leaders in particular traditionally gravitate toward cerebral and task-oriented leadership, what ELVIS calls "intellectual challenge." But that is just one of the seven ELVIS elements. What's more, there is a strong and growing movement for greater inclusion and freedom of expression in the workplace that employees and leaders alike "bring their whole selves to work." It's a nice catch phrase for a bumper sticker, but what does it really mean? How can leaders really accommodate it? And is it even a good idea?

Now that you've worked through the ELVIS methodology, you see this phrase through a more complex and practical identity lens. And the benefits of doing so are laced throughout the stories in this book.

Bringing one's "whole self" to work, for example, is seen as being able to unapologetically inhabit one's multiple identities at work and to express those identities in meeting the tasks and challenges at work. Using ELVIS holistically provides leaders with a clear role (experience designer) and pathway (the ELVIS 7) for making this happen with their teams, not to mention introducing the potential for identity growth across those multiple identities in multiple ways. This, of course, means transformative experiences.

To make it easier for experience designers to use ELVIS holistically, I've put the ELVIS Matrix and all the Design Questions in one place online. Visit the companion site for this book at DesigningTransformativeExperiences.com to download these and begin using them right away. There you will also find an ELVIS Matrix app where you can answer the Design Questions online and get ELVIS "scores" automatically on each of the ELVIS 7 based on your answers.

# Conclusion

Endings

*The only gift is a portion of yourself.*

—Ralph Waldo Emerson

ELVIS (the Experiential Learning Variables & Indicators System) boils down to a very simple yet profound strategy for leadership and for living: to place our identities at the edge of discovery, on the frontiers that can be found both beyond us and within us, rather than tucked safely inside a comfort zone, or where our expectations rule all. When we make our identities vulnerable in this way, it empowers us to not only embrace the unknown as a friend, rich with possibilities, but also navigate those harsher changes that life has in store for each of us. Often, these changes come in the form of endings. Friendships, marriages, jobs, projects, careers, our health, explorations, childhood, and other adventures all come with endings built in, designed or not.

One of the harshest endings, which I've mentioned throughout this book in different ways, is death itself. Our own death is, of course, the most transformative experience waiting for each of us. I am often asked how ELVIS helps us deal with and prepare for this ultimate change. This was brought home to me in a very personal way when my friend and teacher Igor Gamow passed away. In the months leading up to it, we would often talk about this looming event. "The world is full of people trying to tell you how to live," he would say. "Where are the people who can tell you how to die?"

My answer in terms of ELVIS is this: death is an event in life, part of our living experience. It is an invitation to finally give away everything we have and everything we are, back to where it all came from. And it is an invitation we all must accept at some point. We do not know the exact nature of this transformation, but in terms of ELVIS, the result of this final experience is to give away our identities, our very Selves.

Certainly for most of us, this is a discomfort zone experience, and yet also one of the most natural things a person can do. People do it every day and always have. If we have embraced the perspectives of ELVIS and made a practice of identifying and enjoining discomfort zone experiences that place us on the frontiers of life, and if we have owned the processes of change that must occur within us, then death is another such experience (albeit a last one) that I believe we can also face with a sense of agency, inquiry, and (if we are blessed) some degree of design.

Just as ELVIS may provide a new perspective on how we die, ELVIS implies a shift in the way we live and the way we lead. By making our identities vulnerable to change, by developing the insights and skills to make transformations intentional and more likely, and by empowering others to do so as well, we are seizing on a new way of being in the world. And we are doing this at a time when the world is seeing a tidal force of rapid change in almost every way, a time when we need to change our ways of being in the world in order to better cherish and preserve it, and each other.

ELVIS asks all of us who we are and who we want to become, and then gives us the tools to make it so. My hope is that you use

ELVIS to forge beautiful identities for yourself and for others in your sphere, and to forge a better, more beautiful, and more durable identity for the world we share.

I'll end this book the same way that I end my workshops, with a simple message that holds the key to life itself: may we all, in the words of Eugene Bell Jr.,

*Aspire to Inspire before We Expire*

- For brevity, some sections of the original draft of this book were moved online. I encourage you to explore the companion site for this book at DesigningTransformative-Experiences.com. There you can find additional topics and continued discussions on ELVIS Experience Design Leadership and additional bibliographic citations and references.
- You can also find more information about the social science foundations and research methodologies behind ELVIS, including summaries, references, and suggestions for further reading.
- Finally, please visit the Transformative Experience Forum at DesigningTransformativeExperiences.com to share your own stories and questions about Transformative Experience Design with others. Join the community of ELVIS users and continue your journey.
- All of the stories contained in this book are based on real people and actual events. Some of the names, events, locations, and other details have been anonymized to protect individual privacy where needed and to honor nondisclosure agreements with certain organizations I work with.

Acknowledgments

Naturally, no body of work or book like this is possible without the help of others. I celebrate the fact that I've had many hundreds of excellent collaborators and supporters in this journey. The list is long since this book is based on nearly two decades of work. Some of these individuals have worked deeply with me on the questions and answers raised in this book. Others may only partially know of their importance, through their support and/or our projects together that have contributed to my larger work.

Jane Goodall and the Jane Goodall Institute have taught me what tireless hope and passion really mean. Lucy Sanders and Catherine Ashcraft at the National Center for Women & IT (NCWIT) collaborated with me on organizational change leadership with companies all over the world. Daniela Neuendorf at the Bayer Foundation championed and sponsored my work designing transformative experiences with international teens for many years. Sarah Wolman from the Merck Foundation and later with Lego sponsored my transformative experience research in Kenya and Tanzania, Africa, and my international transformative experience conference with over 400 attendees from five countries. Shaun Harner, Jan Bretz, and Randy Bretz at TEDx Lincoln recognized and helped me synthesize this work into something powerful and accessible. Iza Msuya at Trek-2-Kili in Tanzania was my ambassador and co-philosopher through many long African nights where we didn't know how it was all going to turn out. My collaborators on research exploring narrative and team leadership in science education, including the NASA Astrobiology Institute (Daniella Scalice), Bonnie McClain (no relation), Gary Coulter, John Charles, and the crew of STS 107, inspired us all. Sandra Evers-Manly and Cheryl Horn at the Northrop Grumman Foundation, along with Michelle Peters at the Zero-G Corporation, sponsored and collaborated with me on investigating the surreal experience of free-fall micro-G simulation flights, resulting in a most excellent film. My brother Sean McLain, who founded ACME Industrial Imagination, codirected most of my documentary films exploring identity through extraordinary experiences. Kim Vorath, Irene Kendall, and Melissa Vincent at Apple sponsored and collaborated with me on organizational change leadership. Aliza Benach and Sal Cucchiara at Morgan Stanley sponsored and intrepidly led diversity, equity, and inclusion efforts with me and NCWIT for many years. And of course the team at BK Publishing—led by my wise and insightful editor, Charlotte Ashlock—who ultimately saw the promise of this book and opened the gateways from me to you. Thank you all!

# About the Author

**Brad McLain** is a social scientist interested in the nature and psychology of identity development, learning, and leadership. He is the director of the Center for STEM Learning at the University of Colorado Boulder and director of corporate research at the National Center for Women in Information Technology, where he routinely works closely with companies including Apple, Google, Morgan Stanley, and dozens of others on the subjects of identity, inclusive culture construction,  and change leadership. Before that, he served two terms on the board of directors for the Jane Goodall Institute and was the US chair of Goodall's Roots and Shoots Leadership Committee. He has served as principal investigator and researcher on numerous federal, foundation, and privately funded programs, resulting in frequent collaborations with state and federal government agencies, corporations, nonprofits, and private organizations. Before that, McLain was an educational researcher at the Space Science Institute, a NASA educational lead for the Space Shuttle Program as well as NASA's Office of Biological and Physical Research and NASA's Science Mission Directorate, and was a social science researcher at the National Center for Atmospheric Research. He is also an accomplished filmmaker, having produced and directed three documentary features and dozens of short films. McLain lives in Boulder, Colorado, with his two children.

# Berrett–Koehler
## Publishers

**Berrett-Koehler** is an independent publisher dedicated to an ambitious mission: *Connecting people and ideas to create a world that works for all.*

Our publications span many formats, including print, digital, audio, and video. We also offer online resources, training, and gatherings. And we will continue expanding our products and services to advance our mission.

We believe that the solutions to the world's problems will come from all of us, working at all levels: in our society, in our organizations, and in our own lives. Our publications and resources offer pathways to creating a more just, equitable, and sustainable society. They help people make their organizations more humane, democratic, diverse, and effective (and we don't think there's any contradiction there). And they guide people in creating positive change in their own lives and aligning their personal practices with their aspirations for a better world.

And we strive to practice what we preach through what we call "The BK Way." At the core of this approach is *stewardship,* a deep sense of responsibility to administer the company for the benefit of all of our stakeholder groups, including authors, customers, employees, investors, service providers, sales partners, and the communities and environment around us. Everything we do is built around stewardship and our other core values of *quality, partnership, inclusion,* and *sustainability.*

This is why Berrett-Koehler is the first book publishing company to be both a B Corporation (a rigorous certification) and a benefit corporation (a for-profit legal status), which together require us to adhere to the highest standards for corporate, social, and environmental performance. And it is why we have instituted many pioneering practices (which you can learn about at www.bkconnection.com), including the Berrett-Koehler Constitution, the Bill of Rights and Responsibilities for BK Authors, and our unique Author Days.

We are grateful to our readers, authors, and other friends who are supporting our mission. We ask you to share with us examples of how BK publications and resources are making a difference in your lives, organizations, and communities at www.bkconnection.com/impact.

Dear reader,

Thank you for picking up this book and welcome to the worldwide BK community! You're joining a special group of people who have come together to create positive change in their lives, organizations, and communities.

## What's BK all about?

Our mission is to connect people and ideas to create a world that works for all.

Why? Our communities, organizations, and lives get bogged down by old paradigms of self-interest, exclusion, hierarchy, and privilege. But we believe that can change. That's why we seek the leading experts on these challenges—and share their actionable ideas with you.

## A welcome gift

To help you get started, we'd like to offer you a **free copy** of one of our bestselling ebooks:

### www.bkconnection.com/welcome

When you claim your **free ebook**, you'll also be subscribed to our blog.

## Our freshest insights

Access the best new tools and ideas for leaders at all levels on our blog at ideas.bkconnection.com.

Sincerely,

Your friends at Berrett-Koehler

Certified

Corporation